The Lodge Secretary

The Lodge
Secretary

CHARLES J. CARTER

Lewis Masonic

Further books by the same author
The Director of Ceremonies
The Lodge Almoner
The Inner Guard and Deacons
The Wardens, The Chaplain, The Immediate Past
    Master & The Past Masters

All references to the Book of *Constitutions* refers
to the 1989 impression

British Library cataloguing in Publication Data
    Carter, Charles J.
    The Lodge Secretary
    1. Great Britain. Freemasons. Lodges.
    I. Title 366'.10941

First published 1991
Reprinted 1994, 2001
This impression 2007

ISBN (10) 0 85318 183 7
ISBN (13) 978 0 85318 183 5

Published by Lewis Masonic

an imprint of Ian Allan Publishing Ltd,
Hersham, Surrey KT12 4RG.
Printed in England by Ian Allan Printing Ltd,
Hersham, Surrey KT12 4RG.

Code: 0705/3

Visit the Lewis Masonic website at
www.lewismasonic.co.uk

Contents

THE LODGE SECRETARY

Quick Reference Section

The section has been written for easy reference to a shortened version of instructions and rules applying to the assistance most generally required by lodge secretaries.

INDEX

About the Author

Charles James Carter was initiated into the Three Pillars Lodge No 4923 in May 1962, became Master in 1971 and Secretary the following year. In 1971 he became Founding Secretary of the Plantagenets Lodge No 8409 in the Province of Kent and Master in 1973. He served the office of Preceptor and Director of Ceremonies for ten years.

In 1977 he was promoted to Provincial Grand Deputy Director of Ceremonies a rank he was to hold for ten years before being promoted to Assistant Provincial Grand Master (West Kent) in 1987.

He is a member of several lodges and Chapters in Kent including the West Kent Provincial Grand Stewards' Lodge No 8565 (eight years as Director of Ceremonies); he was a founder and the secretary of the Fiennes Cornwallis Lodge No 9279, the executive Lodge for the Province of West Kent. He was appointed to the rank of past Assistant Grand Director of Ceremonies in 1981 and promoted to Past Senior Grand Deacon in 1988. He is a Past Grand Standard Bearer in the Royal Arch.

He is the current secretary of the Quatuor Coronati Correspondence Circle Limited, London, where he is responsible for the worldwide operations of the Correspondence Circle of the Quatuor Coronati Lodge, the premier Lodge of Research in the world, of which he was elected a full Member in 1992.

Acknowledgement
The author wishes to place on record his appreciation of the assistance rendered to him by the Grand Secretary, R.W. Bro. Commander. M.B.S. Higham, Royal Navy, PJGW in reading the contents of this book and for his helpful suggestions in the clarification and amplification of certain chapters.

Chapter 1:

The Official Role

The Book of *Constitutions* states in Rule 104(a) that the office of Secretary is a regular office in the lodge which means that upon his Installation the Master MUST appoint a Secretary. Without that appointment being made the lodge is not regular.

Few would deny that in most lodges the Secretary is the hub around which the lodge revolves. That his day to day involvement in the administration of all matters connected with its smooth running bring him into contact with all the members and thereby he is automatically looked upon as a figure of knowledge, a source of advice and an authority on masonic matters.

His statutory duties are connected with ensuring that returns are made to Grand Lodge of the Installation meeting as well as an Annual return of members. In Provinces and Districts he will have an additional duty to perform in completing an Annual return for that authority as well.

He has the added duty of ensuring that the Master is advised of the correct manner in which the various rules of Grand Lodge are correctly interpreted and obeyed and that the meetings of the lodge are correctly called and that the summons for the meetings are accurately and statutorily correct.

Much of the planning for the masonic year which will include the orderly progress of candidates for the various degrees will fall to his administrative ability. In many lodges the work to be undertaken is decided by the Committee of Management, in others the Master will look to Brother Secretary to advise him of the ideal plan of work for the coming year.

The office of Secretary is undoubtedly a role to be undertaken by a caring, unflappable and genial member whose experience has given him an insight into a wide range of masonic occurrences over a span of many years.

Is this paragon made or born? Every brother appointed to this office brings both strengths and weaknesses. This book is designed to support his strengths and advise and teach him how to overcome any weaknesses there may be in the knowledge he possesses.

It is hoped that this book will serve as a useful aid to advise on the rare and unusual events which from time to time confront him and which he finds are outside his experience thus far.

To the experienced Secretary who may find some items which are explained at length well within his learning curve and current knowledge we would ask him to reflect upon his first appointment as Secretary when almost everything he tackled was new and perhaps a little daunting.

May he remember the helping hands which guided him, and perhaps understand that the author in writing this book has the very new and inexperienced Secretary very much in mind and bear with some explanations which may appear simple in content to the knowledgeable but a minefield to the inexperienced and unwary.

Chapter 2:

Thinking Through the Duties
of the Office

It is generally agreed that the 'lodge year' starts when the new Master is Installed, such Installation is of course most usually undertaken by his predecessor in office.

Assuming that this is so we shall assume that your appointment commences at this meeting which would be the usual case.

The change of secretary is usually a small landmark in the history of the lodge for the office tends to be, by virtue of its considerable involvement within the life of the lodge, an office which is held for a number of years by the incumbent so appointed.

It is usual although not in any sense mandatory for the outgoing secretary to have prepared the Installation return, ready for the new Master to sign some as soon as possible after he has assumed the chair of the lodge and certainly on the night of that Installation.

This form should be despatched to Grand Lodge as quickly as possible after the meeting for the reason that until it is received and duly recorded by Grand Lodge the brethren named therein will possibly not be allowed to attend the Grand Lodge Quarterly Communications.

Without this name being thus recorded Brother Junior Warden will be unable to gain admission should he so wish especially if this should be the first occasion that he has assumed the office of Warden in a lodge.

The recording of the new officers of the lodge will be your first task when the meeting is over so that a permanent record is kept of the various offices in the lodge which its members have held during their membership.

Such information may well be required by future generations in the event of a query arising or if such facts are required when a history of the lodge is being prepared at some future time.

The minutes of the Installation meeting just attended must occupy Brother Secretary's immediate thoughts once the meeting is over.

Usually the recording of the events at an Installation meeting take on a similar form each year and a quick reference to the format used by previous secretaries will assist you considerably in this respect.

The forward-thinking secretary will invariably have a spare copy of last year's minutes available for reference during the meeting which can be altered or amended as required to provide an accurate and up to date record of the occurrences at this year's Installation meeting.

The preparation of the summons for the first meeting of the new master's year will be Brother Secretary's next task.

As the interval between meetings must be a minimum of a month the secretary usually but not always has a few day's breathing space to get the various items together including the details relating to any specific item, for example a Candidate for Initiation.

A good working relationship with your printer is essential if you are to achieve target dates for despatch to and receipt from this essential aid to the efficient running of your lodge affairs and administration.

Where a lodge summons does not include a list of members complete with their addresses it is advisable, once a year, to arrange for such a list to be printed and distributed to all the members. Also send a copy to the reporting base through whom you operate be it London, a Province or a District.

The organisation of the meetings of the Management Committee of the lodge by whatever local name it is known is an important ingredient of the efficient lodge operation.

You should ensure the members who serve on such a committee are given at least three weeks notice of any such meeting and are sent a full agenda of the items to be discussed.

You will of course have ensured that the Master has agreed to your suggested date prior to announcing it by a calling notice.

Candidates and their various proposers and seconders will also require a letter to be written to them advising of the date and time of the meeting as well as its venue, for the purpose of interviewing such prospective new members seeking admission into the lodge either by initiation or by joining.

Brother Treasurer must of course also be available for such an important meeting of the administrative side of the lodge.

It is sometimes the case that the handling of the Management Committee meeting is left in the capable hands of Brother Assistant

Secretary but if this is so in your lodge, always remember that this is a delegated duty and that the ultimate responsibility is yours as the officially appointed and regular officer of the lodge.

Brother Assistant Secretary is an adjunct to brother secretary and cannot replace him unless so invested by the Master of the lodge, when of course he himself becomes brother secretary.

The lodge year requires much planning and organisation. This can most satisfactorily be achieved if a draft plan is put together and presented to the Master for his approval, after which the Management Committee can give their agreement.

This type of forward thinking not only involves a greater number of brethren but also makes the members of the lodge feel more committed and responsible for what is to occur as well as a duty to participate in and support that involvement.

Generally speaking decisions regarding the running of the lodge are more easily accepted and implemented when taken in committee rather than being received as a fait accompli directive from 'on high'!

The ability of Brother Secretary to answer any question on masonic regulations, etiquette or procedures instantly appears to the onlooker to be a prerequisite to such appointment.

Such however is certainly not the case. What is required is the ability to know where to find those answers and to be able to advise questioning brethren if necessary of the right path to take to obtain correct information.

The wise secretary is not the brother who can answer every diverse question immediately and without hesitation for that individual will certainly make many a mistake during his term of office.

Thought, care and consideration are essential if enquiring brethren are to feel a sense of trust and confidence in their lodge secretary.

The guiding hand, the helpful suggestion and on occasions the shoulder to lean on are all needed during the course of any masonic year. On occasions perhaps even a tactful word of advice not asked for when a brother may perhaps be stepping outside due bounds.

Any, and frequently all, newly installed Masters require their confidence boosting from time to time during their year in office.

It is a feature of our masonic teaching system that great emphasis is placed upon ritualistic ability and great stress is placed upon the ability of the Master to conduct 'perfect' ceremonies.

Such however cannot be said of the training given to the Master-elect in the general governing of the lodge in all its facets.

This is where Brother Secretary will need all his experience to provide, when required, such guidance and help but without ever appearing to tell the Master what to do no matter how much on occasions, this might appear to be the right course of action.

A lodge operates by virtue of its Warrant, this fact is known to every member of the lodge for it is explained to him on the night of his Initiation, but what is frequently not realised is that the Warrant is quite specific in its detail regarding from where the lodge may operate, ie, its home.

Such details are contained not only on the Warrant itself but also in the by-laws of the lodge and any change to such a meeting place will necessitate an alteration in the by-laws.

Brother Secretary will find that when he treads this very occasional path it is full of pitfalls for the unwary. This book has therefore set out the steps to be taken in an easy to follow section later in chapter fourteen.

Secretaries come in all shapes and sizes both in abilities and in temperament, of this there can be no doubt. What then is regarded as the ideal secretary if such a person exists?

Possibly the answer is a brother who can communicate at all levels, has an endless amount of tact, who has time for everyone, can answer the same question for the seventh time of asking without showing raised adrenalin, and perhaps above all can smile. One to whom any and everyone will turn knowing that they can rely totally on his professional approach, his knowledge, ability and experience to provide the correct answer to the problem confronting them.

Such qualities are achieved by patience, a desire to help and the ability when necessary to direct action along a more beneficial course than might otherwise be the case.

One facet which is often overlooked by a secretary is that the day will surely arrive albeit sometime in the future when his replacement will need to be chosen.

It is the caring thoughtful secretary who recognises this fact well before other members of the lodge are calling for his replacement.

To achieve high standards in a lodge in the department of administration takes time and the transmitting of knowledge cannot be achieved overnight or in the space of even one or two years.

It is the wise secretary therefore who plans his retirement from office with the same detail and care that he has shown to all his assignments whilst in office.

Generally some three years before his anticipated departure he should speak with the Master and suggest to him (after consultation with the other senior past masters) that Bro . . . be appointed as Assistant Secretary.

This would then allow this new brother to take over slowly many of the repetitive actions required during the lodge year.

Reading the minutes of the lodge could well be a starting point, as well as the task of drafting the next summons.

Then if necessary show him where his draft requires amendment thus building the knowledge of the new man in a step by step process.

It is sometimes the case that after relinquishing the office of secretary, the previous holder will take the subordinate office of Assistant Secretary for a further year or so in order that the newly appointed Secretary may have a readily available source of knowledge should he so require.

Chapter 3:

The Lodge Summons

There can scarcely be a single facet of the many duties of Brother Secretary which contains opportunities to fail and in some cases to fail badly, than those connected with the lodge summons.

In other chapters of this book the various items which can and frequently do require to be mentioned within the confines of the summons are dealt with at length.

In this chapter it is intended to deal with the purpose and general requirements of items which need to appear in the summons in order that brethren who are members are given the maximum opportunity to participate in all the happenings of their lodge.

The first and perhaps most obvious features of a summons is that it should, indeed must, state the date, venue and time of the meeting.

Although the Book of *Constitutions* does not legislate a specified period for the summons to be despatched to a member prior to the date of the meeting it would be a wise secretary who advised his members at least three weeks prior to the meeting.

The reason for so doing is obvious, for the earlier a member is advised of a meeting the greater is the probability of him attending.

The agenda for the meeting should contain the work which the Master has agreed shall be conducted.

It should be remembered at this point that it is the Master not Brother Secretary who shall decide upon the work to be conducted at any meeting of the lodge.

It is also a wise Master who discusses and takes advice both from the secretary as well as the Past Masters of the lodge before reaching a final decision on the format of each meeting.

Clearly it is the duty of the secretary to keep an accurate record of the progression of candidates through the three degrees and thereby ensure an orderly build up to each meeting.

Surprisingly there is no requirement at all for a number of the items which are seen as regular features in the majority of lodge summonses. The names of the officers, the dates of the meetings and of the lodge (other than that to which the summons specifically refers) and virtually all the other miscellany of information constantly seen in most summonses may be helpful but are not mandatory.

Why then is such information provided? The answer presumably is simply to inform, advise and generally ensure that the affairs of the lodge are easily available for all the members at a glance without the need for searching.

Thus we quickly realise that the summons falls into two quite clear sections.

Firstly those things which are mandatory and must be done, and secondly the advisory items which are left to the discretion of the lodge and its administrator(s).

What then are those things which are mandatory? Clearly all matters relating to the admission into the lodge of a new member be he an initiate, joining member, rejoining member, or an honorary member. The precise date for dealing with each of these categories is dealt with at length in another chapter.

Changes in by-laws are another category for mandatory inclusion on the lodge summons, as are alterations in subscriptions rates, initiation fees, joining and rejoining fees.

Notice of a dispensation should be included in the printed summons and that dispensation must be read as soon as the lodge is opened.

The names of candidates for initiation, passing and raising must also be included in the summons for the meeting at which any of these ceremonies takes place.

It is perfectly permissible to make a combined statement which can cover an unclear situation, ie 'to pass two of the three named brethren'.

Do remember if you use this type of general statement that you must subsequently inform your reporting base of what actually occurred at the meeting in order that the records of both Grand Lodge and Provincial or District Grand Lodge are accurate.

Things which can be included of course cover a multitude of items from the presentation of a Grand Lodge Certificate to the reading of the minutes of a previous meeting, to the collection of alms, to take the risings and many more but these are not mandatory requirements and if a lodge should choose to omit any or all of them they would not be wrong, just different.

A summons no matter whether it be a single sheet of paper or a multipage, multicolour tome has a basic message to communicate which is to tell the brethren of the lodge that there is a meeting, where and when it will take place, and what it is intended to undertake at that meeting.

The following chapters of this book will endeavour to cover all the occasions when special attention is required in dealing with an item of particular importance albeit that it may occur only once in a hundred years in the life of the lodge

Chapter 4:

The Installation Return

The purpose of the installation return (form LP & A4) is simple. It is to advise Grand Lodge of the name of the master and wardens of the lodge for the ensuing year. It is also used as a confirmation of a brother's masterships when Grand Lodge are processing applications for London Grand Rank, London Grand Chapter Rank, Senior London Grand Rank, and Senior London Grand Chapter Rank. Similarly they are thoroughly checked when a brother is recommended for Grand Rank in either Craft or Royal Arch.

It also confirms the names of the Past Masters of and in the lodge. Why then should Grand Lodge require this information?

The answer is very simple indeed. Any brother who has been or is a master of a lodge or is a current warden is entitled to attend the Quarterly Communications of Grand Lodge and the means by which Grand Lodge can be aware of those so entitled to attend is by means of the installation return, upon which all such names are listed and filed by lodge number.

A quick reference by the scrutineer will establish the validity of the person so presenting himself at the porch of Grand Lodge and his acceptance or rejection by the scrutineer will determine his entry into or departure from that Quarterly Communication.

It is hoped that this simple explanation will bring home to Brother Secretary the great importance of completing the installation return as quickly as possible after the installation meeting and sending it without delay to Grand Lodge.

Should this action not be taken speedily a situation could arise whereby a newly appointed Junior Warden might present himself for admission and be quite correctly refused entry if his name were not so recorded in the records of Grand Lodge at Freemasons' Hall.

It is the wise Secretary who retains a copy of the Installation return from the previous year. Such diligence will enable an accurate and speedy completion of the new return with the addition of the Past Master who has just stood down from office as the last Past Master shown on the return and the newly Installed Master and his Wardens in the box at the top front of the return.

On the back of the form should be recorded the names and dates of any Past Master who has been omitted for the first time together with the reasons for such omission (ie resignation, death, election as an honorary member, or exclusion) together with the date thereof.

Let us now start to fill in the form from the very beginning, commencing at the top of the first page. Here we find the requirement to enter the name and number of the lodge in the spaces provided.

On the next line should be entered the meeting place of the lodge.

Next we move down the form to where the master's qualification is requested and this requires an answer to one of two questions, ie has he either served as a master or warden before, in which case the lodge number must be entered together with the year he held that office, or as a warden of the lodge of which he has now become master? Obviously, only a lodge under the English Constitution can qualify him.

There is a third alternative which is seldom used but nevertheless is occasionally brought into being where either unfortunate or unexpected circumstances occur.

Rule 109 of the Book of *Constitutions* states that a warden must serve for one complete year before becoming eligible for election as master of the lodge.

It can sometimes be the case that a Warden is not appointed and invested at the installation meeting but at the meeting following thus making his tenure of office shorter than the full year.

In such a case and where the circumstances are acceptable a dispensation may be granted either by the Grand Master or in a Province or District by a Provincial or District Grand Master.

If such a case should prevail in your lodge the date of the dispensation should be entered on the third line of this box.

Beneath this section come both the christian and forenames (in full) together with the date of the installation of the Master and the investiture of the Wardens.

Where either Warden is not invested the reason should be inserted in the space reserved for the date. The Grand Secretary should be notified of the date of the subsequent investiture as soon as it has taken place.

We now move to the body of the form where the names and initials of the Past Masters' are entered.

This will in most cases be a copying exercise from the previous year with the omission of those who are no longer members for whatever reason and the addition of the brother who was the Master during the past year.

It is important that the year of the mastership of each brother is entered together with the lodge number in which he served as master.

This is particularly important if you are placing a new name on the list being that of a brother who has joined your lodge during the past year.

It is most important that you DO NOT include honorary members, so if your lodge during the past year has elected one of your members to this worthy position please be sure that he is not included in this section but that his name and details are removed for inclusion on the back page of this form (more on this later).

Turning now to the reverse of the form we reach the second section where, as mentioned earlier we include for the first time those members who have been omitted from the body of the return for reasons of resignation, death, honorary membership or exclusion.

It is important that both the reason for the omission and the date are filled in accurately and clearly, the lodge minute book will reflect such action being taken be it happy or sad.

A last quick check to see that everything adds up correctly should now be made. The total number of Past Masters shown on the form both front and back must equal those shown on last year's return PLUS the Master for last year and any newly joined Past Masters.

It matters not which section they are in, the total numbers should still add up and this is a simple method of checking your own work.

The last section of the installation return is where the confirmation that the information supplied is accurate and is signed first by the newly installed Worshipful Master whose address should be appended.

The date should be stated on which the form was signed.

Brother Secretary is last to sign the return which together with his completion of the address section together with his telephone number completes this form except for the small box in which has to be stated whether or not there has been a change of Secretary.

This is most important for it will indicate either a change or status quo situation on the Grand Lodge computerised records which determine the postings to lodge secretaries throughout the course of the normal lodge year.

The newly appointed Secretary who neglects to complete this box will find all the information which should be sent to him being sent to his predecessor with, it is suspected, not a little annoyance.

Finally get the form in the post as quickly as possible to Grand Lodge. If you can manage it on the way home from the installation meeting so much the better.

Chapter 5:

The Annual Return to Grand Lodge

The Annual Return of Members is required by Grand Lodge in accordance with Rule 146 of the Book of *Constitutions* and must be rendered within one month of the end of the subscription year if the lodge meets in London or a Province and three months if the lodge meets elsewhere.

During the past five years computerised returns have been produced by Grand Lodge and sent to lodge secretaries for them to check and agree or otherwise and then return with the remittance due to Grand Lodge on behalf of each member.

Clearly if the secretary has been efficient with his recording and form filling throughout the year the checking of this document and its subsequent return complete with a cheque covering the annual dues should be but a simple operation.

What then should this document show? Remember that once again a wise secretary will have before him a copy of the last return so that comparison is easily achieved. The return just received should show a situation similar to that which appertained last year with the exception that any new members advised by the secretary will have been added and those advised as having died, resigned, appointed to honorary membership or excluded will be omitted for the first time.

It should be remembered that dues are still payable for a brother who has died, resigned or being excluded during the year.

In order that this return is as accurate as possible it is essential that Brother Secretary plays his part in ensuring that as soon as an initiation has taken place the form for the new member is despatched to Grand Lodge for recording purposes.

It does not benefit the lodge to retain the form until the brother so concerned has been raised. Indeed reference to Rule 164 will show that the form should be sent to the Grand Secretary together with the appropriate fee immediately after the candidate is initiated or the joining or rejoining member is accepted into the lodge.

The use of Grand Lodge form LP & A5 is provided to assist secretaries in giving the information connected with the passing and raising of candidates and should be used as indicated in chapter seven.

What then should be done if the computerised return which you receive does not agree with the facts as you know them to be?

Clearly you should alter the form and adjust the remittance, but do send a note to Grand Lodge pointing out the changes you have made and the reason you believe the records you received are not accurate, together with payment for the correct amount of annual fees due.

You will not necessarily receive a response from Grand Lodge in answer to your query but your comments will be noted and dealt with, of that you may be quite certain.

Do remember the great number of lodges whose secretaries write to Grand Lodge with all sorts of queries, it simply is not possible to reply to each and every query, particularly if they can easily be dealt with.

There are many reasons why differences occur between the records at Grand Lodge and those held by the secretary.

It has to be said that in the vast majority of cases such differences happen because the secretary does not advise Grand Lodge either quickly enough, or at all, of the entry of a new member into his lodge and is then surprised when that name does not appear on the return.

Remember that the annual return is a collation of the events of the past year and Grand Lodge knows only what it is told by you.

If you do not advise them that a brother has died, resigned or been excluded they will obviously include him on the next return and the request for the payment of fees will be higher than it should be because you have not kept them informed.

A good system is to start a record of membership movement immediately after the despatch of the annual return so that events can be logged in chronological order and dated. Thus when the time arrives for the next annual return to be completed you have before you an easy to read record of the membership movement during the past year.

The completion of the annual return has been simplified to such a degree that it should be an easy matter indeed for the secretary to check it in a very short space of time and obtain the necessary remittance from the treasurer to cover that which is due and then return both to Grand Lodge. Remember to include in the spaces provided, the details required for the Lodge Almoner on the reverse of the form. This is a recent addition to enable Grand Lodge to compile an accurate list of all Almoners.

The return is provided in triplicate, the first copy obviously is sent to Grand Lodge. The second copy of the form you receive from Grand Lodge should be sent to your Provincial or District office for their retention. The third copy of the form should be retained by you for your records, duly amended if such be necessary so that you can answer any future question you may receive from Grand Lodge.

A last word on the subject of forms, always ensure that you fill them in clearly and in block letters.

There are more queries originated by bad hand-writing than by any other cause.

Chapter 6:

Registration Form For Candidates

Rules 159 to 164 of the Book of *Constitutions* deal with the admission of a Candidate into the lodge. You will note that the word Initiate has not been used for this is a multi-purpose form and only one aspect of it deals with a Candidate for Initiation; the others being a Joining or a Rejoining member.

Let us look at this form in detail and examine both the questions it asks and the various answers which can be given in its completion.

At the heading is a space for the name of the lodge and its lodge number beneath which is asked the question Meeting at . . . followed by a question asking the person completing the form to state whether the lodge is a London, Provincial or District lodge and if either of the latter of which Province or District the lodge is a constituent member.

The next part of the printed form deals with the particulars of the Candidate. If he be a Candidate for Initiation then he must complete both parts of section 'A' giving the fullest details of himself and his profession or former profession if he be retired. The newly amended registration form introduced in 1991 has an expanded section under the questions asked of the prospective candidate.

The candidate is now asked to make an unqualified declaration that he has not been convicted of a criminal offence or been the subject of disciplinary proceedings before a professional or similar tribunal.

At first reading the depth of the questions asked may appear unduly intrusive to some brethren. Their inclusion has not been agreed without the fullest debate taking place and the approval of Grand Lodge.

If it should be that Brother Secretary finds himself in discussion with a prospective proposer or seconder of a candidate for Freemasonry in regard to these new questions, he would be well advised to mention the very high standards we set, not only for ourselves but for all who join or wish to join our order. Only those who can meet these high standards should be recommended.

The notes issued by the Grand Secretary's office cover the reasons for these new and searching questions being asked.

Where Candidates for Joining or Rejoining are concerned they need only complete one part of section 'A'.

The requirements are for the name and number of his lodge or former lodge if he be a Joining member together with his rank and year as master should that be applicable.

Where a candidate for Joining comes from another Grand Lodge its name must be clearly stated on this form and the details contained in Rule 163 (e) MUST BE COMPLIED WITH BEFORE THE BALLOT IS TAKEN.

Section 'B' of this form deals with the certificates of the proposer, seconder, master and secretary and it is most important that these certificates are completed in full and with totally correct information.

The particulars contained in the form, including the certificate which is signed by the master, MUST be read in lodge immediately before the ballot is taken. This is stated very clearly on the form and the secretary who omits to read the details is in serious breach of his duty to his office and the lodge.

The last part of this form is the certificate to be signed by Brother Secretary himself and this certifies that the application form complete with the master's certificate was read prior to the ballot being taken and the candidate thereby admitted a member of the lodge by initiation, joining or rejoining.

On the reverse Brother Secretary should insert his own name and address and send the completed form together with the remittance applicable to Grand Lodge in order that the new member's details are correctly entered in their books.

Once again it is recommended that this action is taken as soon as possible after the meeting at which the brother becomes a member.

Chapter 7:

Grand Lodge Certificates

Form LP & A5 is provided by Grand Lodge for the purpose of applying for a Grand Lodge certificate.

It is important that Brother Secretary understands that this form is used ONLY for brethren whose names have already been registered and recorded and for whom registration fees have been paid. It is also a requirement that this form be transmitted to Grand Lodge IMMEDIATELY after the brother concerned has been raised.

It will be remembered that Brother Secretary was earlier advised to despatch to Grand Lodge the application form once the brother had been initiated.

This request for a Grand Lodge certificate will be more speedily dealt with if the former application form was sent immediately after the initiation took place.

Rule 174 (a) states quite clearly the requirements set out by Grand Lodge in this matter.

What is frequently not appreciated is that a special Grand Lodge certificate can, under certain circumstances, be issued after a brother has taken his first or second degree and that such a certificate once issued can be exchanged for one of a higher degree without charge at a later date. Rule 174 (c) confirms.

The presentation of a Grand Lodge certificate is dealt with under the same rule sub section (d).

Such certificate must, upon presentation, be signed in open lodge by the brother to whom it is issued and the fact recorded in the minutes of the meeting.

If such a certificate should become lost or destroyed a replacement may be issued upon payment of the appropriate fee.

Chapter 8:

Dispensations

A dispensation is an authority from the issuing power to alter, change or otherwise counteract a rule, regulation or instruction. Reference to the Book of *Constitutions* will show that a dispensation can be issued for the majority of the rules and regulations contained within its covers.

Instances occur in most lodges whereby a dispensation is sought to alter or change something which is fixed. In most cases this will be the day of a lodge or chapter meeting. Occasionally a brother will perhaps overlap his mastership of two lodges under the English Constitution and require a dispensation for this under Rule 115.

To seek a dispensation Brother Secretary should write to his reporting base be that Grand Lodge in the case of London lodges or to his Province or District in the case of lodges outside London. Included in his submission must be a clear explanation why a departure from the established and existing rules or by-laws is required.

It is an oddity of Rule 115 that a District Grand Master can issue dispensations for a brother to hold the chair of master in two lodges consecutively or for an overlapping period whereas a Provincial Grand Master cannot, this authority being retained by Grand Lodge itself.

In the case of a dispensation for a duality of mastership it is essential that the brother so concerned is installed into the chair of one lodge before the application is made for a dispensation to allow him to be installed into another chair.

Grand Lodge will inspect their records to ascertain that the brother for whom the dispensation is required has already been installed into the chair of King Solomon. This occurs more often than might be appreciated particularly where and when emergencies arise.

Brother Secretary should acquaint himself with the many and various reasons why and when a dispensation may be sought.

This can be achieved without need of study by simply referring to the item 'Dispensations' in the index of the Book of *Constitutions* where he will find dispensations can be granted as has already been stated for a very wide range of occasions and events, from an Initiation under the age of twenty-one years to holding a Provincial or District Grand Lodge meeting outside the boundary of the Province or District so applying. It should be remembered that a dispensation can only be issued to cover those cases provided for in the Book of *Constitutions*. If the reason for which you are seeking a Dispensation does not appear under the listing shown in the Book of *Constitutions* then none can be issued. Should Brother Secretary be in any doubt he should, in a Province or District consult the Provincial or District Grand Secretary. For lodges meeting within the London area the London Department at Freemasons' Hall will assist either by telephone, letter or personal visit.

There is usually a fee to be paid for the work undertaken in supplying a dispensation to a lodge.

Just occasionally a Province or District will grant a dispensation free of charge to a lodge or chapter within its authority if the normal meeting day of that lodge or chapter falls on the same day as the annual Provincial or District Grand Lodge or Provincial or District Grand Chapter meeting.

Dispensations must always be read immediately after the lodge or chapter has been opened and before the minutes of the previous meeting or any other item is dealt with.

Such dispensation must be recorded in the minutes of the meeting held by virtue of that dispensation.

If a regular meeting falls upon Christmas Day, Good Friday, a Sunday, or a public holiday, the meeting may be held not more than seven days before or after, as the Master shall direct and without the need for a dispensation.

Otherwise, a dispensation can be given only if the revised date is not more than twenty-eight days before or after the normal date.

Chapter 9:

Exclusion of a Member

If Rule 181 is examined it will be found that given here in fine detail is the precise procedure to be followed if a lodge wishes to exclude one of its members for whatever reason.

One reason when this rule can be invoked is where the by-laws of a lodge allow for the exclusion of a member for the non-payment of fees for a period less than the statutory two years as stated in Rule 148.

The exclusion of a member is a serious matter and should never be entered upon without the greatest care and consideration of other methods of bringing home to the member concerned the feelings of his fellow brethren in regard to his behaviour either specifically or generally.

If after due consideration it is decided to proceed with the exclusion of a member then the details of Rule 181 MUST be followed very carefully and if after such a vote is taken the result proves positive then the reporting base of the lodge must be informed accordingly as well as Grand Lodge itself.

Exclusion from one lodge does not mean exclusion from any other lodge, chapter or any other masonic body. The behaviour of one member should never be allowed to interfere with the happiness and enjoyment of the majority.

Chapter 10:

Losing Touch with a Member

It can occasionally happen that despite all reasonable care to avoid it a member will move home and a break with the lodge will be made.

The first indication that Brother Secretary will have is when a letter or a summons to a meeting is returned, marked 'Gone away'. What then should be the action he should take?

Clearly there are various actions which immediately spring to mind from enquiring first of the brother's proposer and seconder of his new address to following up the letter with a personal visit to see whether a forwarding address has been made known to a neighbour.

Action is required as quickly as possible when such a break occurs for it may well be that the brother concerned is ill, or has been taken to hospital and no one is aware of his current situation or is able to assist him in his possible dilemma.

It is sometimes the case that another brother in the lodge will have the telephone number of the missing brother's workplace and can check from that angle to see if all is well.

It is most important that the other members of the lodge play their part in striving to make contact with the lost brother.

If the treasurer has knowledge of the brother's bank this can be another way of re-establishing contact by means of forwarding a letter via that bank.

Banks are particularly helpful in ensuring that mail sent via them is passed on quickly to their client.

It may well be that another member of the lodge has knowledge of another organisation of which the missing brother is a member such as church, rotary, or a golf club or some other local activity from whom a new address can be gained.

It should never be assumed that because a brother has moved and not advised you of his new address that he has done so quite deliberately.

There are many reasons why you as secretary do not appear to have been advised from the simple reason that a card was sent to you but became lost in the post, to simple forgetfulness even to the point of believing he has already told you of his intended move.

It should always be remembered that moving home is a stressful business and it is quite possible to overlook the advising of someone it was intended to inform.

There are many ways to re-establish contact if you really wish to do so but time is the essence in carrying out the advised exercises, for memories dim as the weeks pass, in the same way as small pieces of paper with new addresses on them become lost or destroyed by friends and previous neighbours.

Chapter 11:

Death of a Lodge Officer

A frequently held belief albeit quite wrongly, is that if an officer of the lodge should die or become unable to execute his office for the remainder of the year, the office cannot be filled until the next installation meeting.

This is quite wrong as reference to Rule 121 will quickly show.

It should be stated quite clearly here that this applies to all lodge officers with the single exception of the Master.

Where an election is required to fill an office (eg Treasurer and Tyler) then such office shall not be filled until that election has taken place and a positive result has been obtained.

What then should be the procedure if one of the regular officers other than the Treasurer or Tyler, let us say the Senior Deacon, should die and how is such a situation covered by the Book of *Constitutions?* Rule 104 (a) states quite clearly who are the regular officers in the lodge.

The Master should appoint without delay another brother to this office and invest him at the next meeting of the lodge even if this should be for one meeting only before the start of the new masonic year with the subsequent installation of a new master.

Chapter 12:

The Warrant of the Lodge

This may seem at first glance a strange chapter to include in a book aimed at secretaries of lodges but it is most important that the information contained herein is understood and applied by all who have the care and concern of the lodge as their primary duty and surely Brother Secretary is first in line where duty is concerned.

We all know that when a lodge is consecrated, the consecrating officer presents to the first master the warrant of the lodge charging him to pass it to his successor when his year as master is over.

The master of a lodge when installing his successor uses such phrases as 'I now pass into your care the Warrant of the lodge. For many years it has been in the hands of worthy and distinguished brethren and in entrusting it to your care I know that it will lose none of its lustre but will be passed to your successor pure and unsullied as you now receive it'.

Why then is this Warrant so important and why is the master so frequently seen to be carrying it into the lodge and why is he often seen to display it either before or immediately after the start of the lodge meeting?

The answer can be found in Rule 101 of the Book of *Constitutions* and it will no doubt come as a great shock to the reader to find that the warrant does not 'belong' to the lodge. The master in fact holds the Warrant in safe custody on behalf of the Grand Master.

The Master (the rule continues) shall produce it at every meeting of the lodge. Hence we can at once appreciate that a meeting at which the Warrant is not available is unconstitutional and cannot be held.

The Master of the lodge is perhaps completely unaware for the entire period of his mastership that he is holding the Warrant in trust for the Grand Master, and it is to be recommended that the master be encouraged to address himself to Rule 101 most carefully before he is installed into the chair of King Solomon.

One oddity of Rule 101 is the unclear statement about 'producing it' and precisely what 'producing it' really meant in practice. This choice of words has caused much discussion for the use of the word 'displaying' might have been more specific. A Master would therefore be acting within the terms of this rule by simply holding the Warrant aloft for the brethren to see for he would indeed have 'produced' it.

It is the case in the majority of lodges that the Warrant is removed from its case displayed in full to the assembled brethren but a lodge which does not conform to this practise should not be criticised providing always that the Warrant was present within the lodge room.

It is perhaps a good exercise for the Master to undertake the complete opening of the warrant case and displaying the warrant fully so that all present can see that they are taking part in a properly constituted and regular meeting of the lodge. This can however wear the Warrant out.

The Warrant is of course the document which gives authority to the lodge in general and the Master in particular to Initiate, Pass and Raise Candidates for Freemasonry — without the Warrant the lodge is not regular and ceremonies must not be performed.

The question is sometimes raised by lay brethren who see the Warrant of a lodge framed and totally 'on show' in a masonic hall: 'How can the master say I place in your hands the Warrant of the Lodge when it is firmly fixed to the wall of the Temple?'

A totally relevant question and one which can only be answered by the questioner allowing a free use of poetic licence, for the phrase used by the Master is one of free licence of the English language and should not be taken too literally.

The author has on occasions heard the same phrase varied to the words 'I now entrust to your care [indicating with his hand its position on the Temple wall] the Warrant of the Lodge'. This covers the situation equally as well and does not offend the 'pure in heart'.

What then is the Centenary Warrant? Can this not be used in place of the lodge Warrant issued when the lodge was consecrated?

The answer to that question is NO and the reason is simple, the Centenary Warrant is the 'official' proof that the lodge has completed an unbroken period of one hundred years of activity and it permits the lodge members to wear a Centenary Jewel of the style and design emblazoned on the Centenary Warrant.

You will of course now appreciate that to try to use the Centenary Warrant in place of the lodge Warrant is completely wrong and should never be permitted, and more to the point the lodge is not regular!

The same comments of course apply equally to a Bicentenary Warrant, the purpose of which is to authorize the wearing of a bar on the Centenary Jewel with the engrossment 'CC' signifying two hundred years of continuous working.

Chapter 13:

Assisting the New Master

The approach to the master's chair is a time of serious thought and much deliberation for the brother who intends to carry out this most important duty to the very best of his ability as well as the satisfaction of the Past Masters and his fellow brethren.

There is much that the secretary can do to smooth the path for the new Master and a meeting some weeks prior to his installation is to be highly recommended.

To benefit both parties to the full it is considered that a one-to-one meeting is likely to prove the most beneficial.

Try to hold this meeting on an evening when both of you have at least three hours to give without prior or post appointments which can interfere with the thought processes of both.

What then are the items which should be discussed at this important meeting?

Listed below are some of the major points which will affect the running of the lodge and the smooth period of mastership which the Master-Elect is seeking to have.

1. The work for the year ahead meeting by meeting — in detail.
2. Meetings of the Lodge Committee during the year.
3. Interviewing of Candidates.
4. The Lodge Finances.
5. Officers selected for the coming year.
6. Special events during the year.
7 Possible changes of dates of meetings.
8. Completing the Installation return.
9. Completing the Annual return.
10. Completing the Provincial or District Annual return.
11. Special items for the lodge summons — if any.
12. The Master's Charity list for the year ahead.
13. Potential list of Speakers at any meetings during the year where this is considered desirable.

14. Advise him of the Brethren giving the addresses.
15. Provide details of the representative attending if any.
16. Ensure he has obtained a Master's apron.
17. Ascertain his list of guests for his installation.
18. Are there any VIP guests attending? Get names and titles.
19. Explain the Festive Board Toast List to him in detail.
20. Discuss and agree the list of Wine Takings.
21. Agree the speakers for the various toasts.
22. Ensure the Master-elect communicates well with the D.C.
23. Explain that proposers of toasts at the Festive Board for each of his meetings during the year should be advised well in advance of those meetings taking place.
24. Above all else ensure that the new Master knows and accepts that he must make such decisions and direct the lodge for the benefit of all the brethren.
25. Let him see that he can call upon your services in any situation which occurs during his year and that you will give him an unbiassed opinion based on your years of experience in the Craft.

It will be seen from the above list that there is indeed plenty of information to impart to a Master-elect and the time will not be wasted if the list given above is dealt with in detail.

It will benefit both the Master-elect and his secretary to have this one-to-one meeting so that the year ahead can be planned in detail and without the need for diverse opinions entering the proceedings during the course of the year.

The most successful years in the history of a lodge are those planned and carried through with meticulous attention to every small detail.

Waiting for the meeting of the lodge to arrive and then rushing around trying to organise in fine detail those things which should have been attended to weeks before shows not only bad planning but also a lack of organisation and thinking ahead which should be the backbone of every good secretary and as we know, the backbone of every good Master is his secretary!

The efficient operation of a lodge by the Master assisted by his Secretary will produce a cohesive partnership of dynamic proportions, to the benefit of the lodge and all of its members.

Chapter 14:

The Lodge By-laws

When a new lodge is formed and subsequently consecrated one of the items contained in the body of consecration agenda is the 'Adoption of the By-laws as recommended by the Founders'. These must of course be approved on behalf of the Grand Master.

What this means in effect is that the by-laws (or the rules by which the new lodge will be governed) become effective from this point onwards.

It is customary these days for the model by-laws as printed by the Grand Secretary's Office to be used with the addition only of the place and days of the meetings (the fees for members) and other various parochial details to be filled into these model By-laws and then submitted for approval to the reporting authority.

In fact what happens of course is that almost invariably the reporting authority has already seen the intended By-laws and if necessary has suggested amendments and alterations where these appeared desirable.

In years past strange By-laws limiting membership of lodges were sometimes included and were approved but this would not now be countenanced.

One of the most recent helpful By-laws has been the ability of lodges to alter their annual fees without the necessity to change the By-laws each time, as used to be the case.

Such amendments to fees require a notice of motion given in open lodge followed by a printed version on the summons at which the vote is to be taken.

Subsequent action to collect such adjusted annual fees may proceed without recourse to higher authority or the reporting authority in whose jurisdiction the lodge or chapter falls.

It will be remembered that on every annual return to Grand Lodge the amount of the annual subscription is requested for record purposes so that Grand Lodge will know, albeit perhaps a year in arrears, the amount of the various subscriptions which the members of every constituent lodge within its overall control has to pay.

The procedures and documentation connected with moving a lodge from one venue to another are probably one of the more complicated areas of administration which a secretary has to cope with in his period of secretaryship.

The work which is required of such a transaction falls into three distinct parts.

First the background work. The acceptance by the masonic hall or venue of your lodge or chapter as an entity (remember that all venues MUST be approved by either the Grand Master or the Provincial or District Grand Master under whose authority they come), and the confirmation of the dates you will require need to be established.

If the dates you require are not available you will require to consult with your members and agree alternative dates before matters can proceed.

Let us assume this has been done and that for the purposes of this exercise you have established both a new home for the lodge and new dates on which you will meet and, lastly and perhaps as important, when that first meeting in the new home will take place.

What should we now do next? Answer move to stage two.

Read Rule 141 of the Book of *Constitutions* which sets out very clearly the action which should now be taken.

A verbal notice of motion, signed by no less than seven subscribing members of the lodge should be given to the effect that the lodge be removed to a new home, such notice of motion can include as well the alteration of the dates and days of the meeting if this is necessary.

This verbal notice is of course usually given by Brother Secretary and recorded in the minutes of the meeting.

On the summons for the next meeting (or for a special meeting called for the sole purpose of considering and finally deciding the motion) for either of which no less than seven days notice must be given, the details should be printed of the notice of motion as stated verbally at the previous meeting.

The motion will not be carried unless two-thirds of the members voting shall be in favour of it and, if carried, shall effect, subject to all necessary approvals, the appropriate alterations in the By-laws of the lodge.

We move now to the third and final stage. The reading of Rule 141 sections (iii), (iv) and (v) will show the actions which should be taken subsequent to the vote having been in favour of the suggested move of the unit from one venue to another.

A last word on By-laws in general; remember that to tie the lodge and thereby its members too tightly into given actions or forms of procedure can prove restrictive to future generations when circumstances and situations may prevail which are different from those appertaining when the By-laws were originally drawn up by the founders of the lodge.

The message is therefore very clear. Try to think ahead and realise you are setting up rules when you draft By-laws for a new lodge and that these should be kept as close to the model By-laws provided for the guidance of new lodges as possible.

Chapter 15:

Honorary Members

Rule 167 of the Book of *Constitutions* clearly states the manner in which the ballot for an honorary member should be conducted, namely by individual ballot and be declared carried unless three or more black balls appear against it.

This of course is just the culmination of the decision of the members that they wish to elect a brother or brethren to this distinction. What then precedes this end result and how does the honorary member fit into the overall pattern of life within the lodge?

It is evident to everyone who attends a consecration of a lodge or chapter that the Consecrating Officer and his team of officers who partake in this unique occasion in the life of the new unit are invariably elected to become honorary members.

Their names frequently appear on the summons of that lodge or chapter until such time as the years have passed and the brethren concerned have left this mortal coil.

To have or not to have honorary members is a distinctly private decision for the members of the lodge or chapter to make and Grand Lodge does not lay down firm and unequivocal rules for the consideration and possible subsequent election of such brethren.

What it does say however is that 'A Lodge shall have the power, after notice placed on the summons, to elect as an Honorary Member any Brother of good standing and worthy of such distinction by reason of his services to the Craft, or to the particular Lodge, who is, or within the previous year has been, a subscribing member of a regular Lodge.'

Clearly therefore making a brother an honorary member is not an action to be taken lightly or without much thought and discussion.

Tactfully Brother Secretary should speak to the prospective honorary member in confidence to make sure that he would be willing to accept such an honour if granted by the membership.

Often those elected to such distinction are Grand Officers and where this occurs, as indeed with all honorary members it is impor-

tant that an annual check is made with each new Masonic Year
Book to ensure that the Grand Officer so elected is still shown and
continues to retain the rank shown on your lodge summons.

It is frequently the case with senior Grand Officer for them to be
promoted to a higher rank and clearly you would not wish your
lodge summons to contain incorrect information.

Grand Lodge sets no limit on the number of honorary members a
lodge may elect since such service warranting this honour does not
usually occur in large numbers.

Being an honorary member brings with it certain privileges and
certain restrictions and these are fully explained in Rule 167.

A clear distinction is shown between those who have been both
members and Past Masters of the lodge and those who have not.

It is important that a brother who is about to be so honoured and
whose membership of the craft is restricted to the lodge who is
about to honour him, is made aware that as in future neither he nor
a lodge will be paying any annual dues to Grand Lodge on his
behalf he will in effect be 'an unattached brother' albeit he is an
honorary member on this one lodge.

The importance of this information being communicated to an
elderly brother should not be minimised for he could quite unwit-
tingly place himself outside the facility to visit other lodges on a frequent basis being restricted as an unattached brother to one visit
only to any lodge under the English Constitution.

Honorary membership is frequently a reward for service to the
lodge over many years and is conferred upon brethren of many
years membership and outstanding service.

Grand Lodge is careful to make the observation that honorary
membership should never be used as a means of accommodating a
brother who can no longer afford to pay his lodge dues.

Chapter 16:

The Lewis

The subject of the status of a Lewis is one of the most frequently misunderstood rules in Freemasonry and this may perhaps be due to the wording used in the first degree tracing board which is quoted hereunder

"Lewis likewise denotes the son of Mason; his duty to his parents is to bear the heat and burden of the day, which they by reason of their age, ought to be exempt from; to assist them in time of need, and thereby render the close of their days happy and comfortable; his privilege for so doing is that of being made a Mason before any other person, however dignified".

The last three lines are without doubt the cause of the belief amongst so many brethren that when a Lewis (the uninitiated son of a mason be he born before or after his father became a mason) presents himself for membership of a lodge he shall by virtue of his being a Lewis be placed in front of all waiting brethren who have been duly balloted and accepted by the lodge.

Such however is most decidedly not the case as reference to the small booklet accompanying the annual issue of the Masonic Year Book will show.

This booklet entitled 'Information for the Guidance of Members of the Craft' states under the heading 'Lewis' the following:

(i) *Description of*
  A Lewis is the uninitiated son of a Mason and it matters not whether the son was born before or after his father became a Mason.
(ii) *Privileges of*
  Where a Lewis is one of two candidates being initiated on the same day he would be the senior for the purpose of the ceremony. He cannot claim precedence over candidates proposed or elected previously to himself and he must take his

place in the usual rotation of any waiting list. Being a Lewis is not grounds for dispensation to enable him to be initiated under the age of 21 (Rule 157, B. of C.).

It will be clearly seen from the above extract from the Grand Lodge booklet precisely the precedence to which a Lewis is entitled, and perhaps equally as important that to which he is not.

Further, an initiate whether or not he is a Lewis, should be seated immediately on the right of the Senior Deacon after the ceremony. He has no precedence in the outgoing procession and no right to any particular seat at the Social Board, though he may be allocated one by custom of the Lodge.

Brother Secretary is strongly advised to have a copy of this small booklet with him at all meetings of the lodge and lodge committees' on which he serves. In particular he should show to a proposer of a Lewis the rules which deal with his particular situation. This will stop any misunderstanding occurring.

Chapter 17:

Changing the Venue

Changing the venue at which a lodge meets can be complex and difficult if not dealt with correctly from the start.

Rule 141 deals with this subject in ample form but for the sake of a secretary whose knowledge may be limited in this field a step by step guide is given hereunder.

For the purpose of this explanation it is assumed that the members have decided that they wish to move and that there is little or no dissension to the proposition.

First, and perhaps most obvious, ensure that the venue to which you intend to move is approved by Grand Lodge or the Provinical or District Grand Lodge responsible for your area and also that the venue can accept you.

Second, make sure that you receive in writing a confirmation of the dates they have agreed with your lodge as satisfactory for the future and more particularly the date on which the new arrangement will commence.

Third, work out the time in terms of meetings of your lodge that you require to be able to complete the various steps so that you are completely certain that you have enough time to allow the necessary legislation to go through the system, both for your own lodge and your reporting authority.

This is of particular importance if you should be moving from one controlling area to another e.g. from London to a Province as in this case both reporting areas will require adequate notice and the receiving area must be willing to accept your lodge into their Province to which end you should obtain an agreement in writing.

Fourth ensure that a properly prepared Notice of Motion signed by seven subscribing members is read on the third rising at your next lodge meeting.

This notice of motion should indicate the address of the new venue, the days it is intended to meet there and, for the information of the brethren of the lodge, the date of the first meeting it is intended to hold at this new venue.

Do remember that any change of venue and possibly a change of days of meeting will necessitate a change of by-laws so this should be included in the notice of motion.

This can be done by adding the words after the detail of the change of venue 'and that by-laws . . . and . . . be altered accordingly'.

Fifth, ensure that the summons for the next meeting contains all the details which you gave in your notice of motion at the previous meeting, including the names of the seven brethren who signed the Notice of Motion.

The words 'Pursuant to the Notice of Motion given at the meeting on . . . to submit, discuss and vote upon the following resolution . . .' should be used as a heading to the written statement on the summons itself.

Sixth, after the vote is taken and for the purpose of this exercise it will be assumed the vote is in favour of the motion. You should communicate the news to your reporting centre and also send a newly-worded alteration to your by-laws to the Grand Secretary or your Provincial or District office to allow them to approve the change.

They will of course also adjust their own records regarding your lodge and its new venue and possible alterations in meeting dates at the same time. Grand Lodge will make such changes as are necessary in the Masonic Year Book.

A word on the subject of changing venues — moving a lodge is always an emotive occasion and it is quite surprising how brethren react to a suggestion made in all innocence and purely for the good of the lodge.

Brethren become attached to the venue where they were initiated and have met for some years and the thought of a new home no matter how much better it might be from all points of view is sometimes totally unacceptable to them.

Never assume that because you or the other Past Masters have an eminently sensible reason for wishing to move your base that you will necessarily receive total and absolute support from everyone in the lodge for it is virtually certain you will not.

Chapter 18:
Ballots for Initiates, Joining or Honorary Members

The word Candidate is most frequently interpreted by a member of the craft to be one who is seeking initiation and this is perhaps understandable even if it is totally incorrect, taken as a single meaning.

The word Candidate refers to anyone who wishes (or is invited in the case of a joining member) to become a member of a lodge, either by initiation, joining, rejoining or by being made an honorary member.

There is frequently much misunderstanding on the subject of taking a conjoint ballot, ie, taking two or three ballots at the same time, the following explanation may assist those who are not sure of the correct procedure.

It is quite in order for a ballot covering any variation of the above-mentioned groupings to be carried out in one ballot. Should there prove to be a negative vote then it is of course mandatory for individual ballots to be undertaken.

Surely, we can hear some of you saying: 'you cannot ballot for a candidate for initiation, a candidate for joining and a candidate for honorary membership in the same ballot!'

Well the answer to that comment is: 'yes you can', although it would be unusual, since all three of the categories which have been mentioned would be unlikely to arise at the same meeting.

Let us now deal with the ballot for the candidates for initiation which is the more general type of ballot we tend to experience in our lodges.

What then are the potential difficulties which can arise in carrying out what appears to be a simple and straightforward piece of administrative procedure?

Let us look at the form which the candidate completes in detail. Has the candidate completed all the sections required of him and equally as important has he signed the form after completing it?

Has the form been signed by his proposer and seconder and have they completed their responsibilities by stating precisely how long they have been acquainted with the candidate?

Does the candidate live or work within the jurisdiction of the masonic authority for your lodge? If not has clearance been obtained from either London, the Province or District in which the candidate resides stating that they have no objection to his candidature?

If no such certificate has been obtained then the ballot cannot proceed because for it to do so would be totally unconstitutional (see Rule 158) the last line of which reads 'A candidate coming within the provisions of this Rule shall not be proposed in open Lodge until the Masonic Authority has replied to the enquiries'.

If the reply is not completely favourable, it would be wise to institute careful enquiries before proceeding further.

Let us assume that all is well and that the details of the candidate can be read in open lodge on the appropriate rising. What then happens after that?

The details of the candidate should be prepared ready for inclusion in the summons for the next regular meeting of the lodge. Details of what this statement should contain are shown in detail in Rule 164 of the Book of *Constitutions*.

In most cases reference to a previous summons will suffice to ensure that you have included all the necessary information about this new candidate.

We now arrive at the point where we are ready to take the ballot in the lodge.

The item being reached on the summons the Master will invariably call upon the secretary to read out the form in detail which should be done with great care, even if it was fully read at the previous meeting.

Brother Secretary must add the statement contained at the base of the form which in fact states that this form has been read and has been signed by the Master to that effect.

In some lodges the Master signs the form in open lodge immediately before the ballot is taken. In others it is done prior to the meeting commencing.

We shall assume that the ballot proves favourable to the candidate.

Here it should be remembered that the only duty the Master has is to declare the ballot either carried or not carried, he should not, indeed must not discuss the ballot by saying for example, 'With the exception of two black balls the ballot is in favour', neither should he use the word 'unanimous'. If it became his custom so to do, then if he omitted the word on any occasion, it would suggest to the brethren that one or more adverse votes had been recorded.

If the lodge has no alternative by-law then the Grand Lodge recommendation of three black balls excluding a candidate appertains (see Rule 165). Brother Secretary should always make certain that the Master knows how many black balls exclude in his lodge. On occasions a Master has been known to order the ballot to be retaken where there has been an adverse vote, 'in case a mistake has been made'? This is quite improper and should never be done.

Now we have arrived at the situation where a potential candidate for initiation has been approved and can be initiated at a meeting convenient to the lodge and the person concerned.

A letter should now be written to the prospective new member advising him of the date of the meeting at which he will be initiated and the approximate time he will be required to present himself.

It does sometimes happen that a lodge will ballot and initiate a candidate on the same day. This can be a situation fraught with potential problems for if the ballot should not prove to be in favour of the candidate then clearly there are two immediate problems.

The first is that of informing of the prospective candidate waiting in the ante-chamber and secondly the total loss of the ceremony from the meeting.

It is always to be recommended that a ballot be taken and the candidate informed in writing of the success or otherwise of that ballot as soon as possible after the meeting has taken place.

Whilst dealing with the subject of potential candidates and their successful or unsuccessful applications for admittance into a lodge, it cannot be stated too strongly that for an objection to a candidate only to be voiced when the ballot is taken shows both a lack of communication on the part of the lodge members and a lack of sensitivity on the part of the member or members so objecting towards the proposer and seconder.

Let us now deal with the ballot for the Joining or Rejoining member. The former is quite a usual occurrence the latter a more rare event.

Clearly the candidate in the former case will have visited the lodge before and as a result of such a visit or visits has found an empathy existing between himself and the brethren hence his request to join as a full member.

The same form requires completion (in different parts) and of course a proposer and seconder are required. The necessity for residential or work place qualifications are deemed unnecessary for this category of application.

The same procedure of reading a form at one meeting and balloting at the next meeting will apply as will the requirement to state that the form was read before the ballot was taken.

It is the practice in some lodges for the brother concerned to be requested to retire from the lodge whilst the ballot is being taken, in others it is the custom to allow him to remain within the lodge room. There would appear to be no ruling on this point. A final word on the joining member, do make sure that Rules 163 and 164 are fully complied with before a ballot is taken, particularly in regard to clearance certificates.

Handling the application of a rejoining member is slightly different for this can often be a past member who has either lapsed for a lengthy period or who has perhaps been working abroad for many years and now wishes to resume membership of his old lodge.

Once again clearance certificates will be required as will a proposer and seconder and a brother who wishes to rejoin his lodge should not assume that simply because he was a member many years ago that there is an automatic guarantee of his being accepted back again after a long absence.

There can well be a totally new membership in the lodge now none of whom either know the brother concerned or wish to have him as a member of 'their' lodge.

Such a situation may not sound very brotherly or masonic but it is democratic and compliance with the Book of *Constitutions* is essential.

Brother Treasurer should make quite sure that any prospective returning brother to the lodge was clear of all dues prior to his departure albeit many years before.

In such circumstances it can be difficult for a rejoining brother after a lengthy break in membership to find brethren who know him well enough to propose and second his candidature.

Ballots for honorary members must be handled in accordance with Rule 167 and the ballot MUST be carried out using a ballot box (a show of hands is not enough). This is a rule and may not be varied no matter how distinguished, much loved or long serving the brother so honoured may be.

Honorary membership brings with it much status and respect but the brother to whom it is being offered, should he so accept must be advised that he can be at a disadvantage if this is the only lodge of which he is a member. For if it should be that this is the only lodge which is paying an annual fee to Grand Lodge for his membership then the acceptance of this honour may well reduce him to the status of an 'unattached brother'.

It is suggested that reading chapter 15 will assist in ensuring that the election of an honorary member is dealt with correctly.

The reading of Rule 127 will also be beneficial.

Chapter 19:

The Annual Return to Provincial or District Grand Lodge

Why is such a return necessary and what is its purpose?

An annual return to the masonic authority directly responsible for the area in which your lodge meets is required for a number of reasons.

First, it is needed so that an accurate assessment can be made of the monies due to the Province or District for the year in question based on a given sum per member.

Second, it is required so that any movement in membership can be accurately checked and recorded, particularly those who have died, resigned or been awarded honorary membership during the year.

Third, that the entry of new members both initiates, joining members and rejoining members can be recorded.

Fourth, that the Provincial or District Grand Master can, with total accuracy, include the details of growth or diminution of the membership of the lodges within his authority in the annual report he makes to the Grand Secretary as required under Rule 77 of the Book of *Constitutions*.

Chapter 20:
Minutes

Those brethren who visit extensively will notice the wide and seemingly quite different versions of minutes of meetings read by Brother Secretary.

Why should this be? Surely minutes are minutes and they should all conform to a similar if not precise set of rules? Is this view correct?

Let us examine the dictionary description of the word 'minutes'.

Although dictionaries vary slightly in their overall description they all use the expression 'to record the proceedings of a meeting'.

Let us take this further, surely if this statement is taken to its fullest extent then the minutes would be as long as the meeting itself!

Time and experience has modified such a widely given statement to a given record of the principal events which occurred at any meeting and certainly to record for posterity the result of decisions taken and votes both for and against any motion which was put forward.

In Masonic lodges other details require to be noted, in particular details of those who have been appointed to a given office, those who have been the recipient of a degree, matters affecting the donation of monies, the agreement to an increase in fees.

The proposers and seconders of motions and candidates must also be noted. Other details which must be recorded are the election of a new Master, Treasurer, and of course a Tyler.

One of the many reasons that the minutes in some lodges stretch out to such an interminable length can usually be associated with the fact that the newly appointed secretary carries on the traditions of the past and then starts to introduce phrases or extra verbiage of his own.

Thus the expansion of the minutes continues from one secretary-ship to another and the records in consequence thereof grow and grow and grow!

There comes a time when a secretary needs to look at what has gone before and perhaps start again from the beginning with a carefully balanced and well thought out set of writings designed to inform and confirm those things which are necessary but without those unnecessary paragraphs of happenings which interest no one and have no need to be recorded.

In the spring of 1989 the author sat through the reading of the minutes of a lodge which lasted twenty-four minutes.

These extended to seven pages of closely typed script and contained virtually every movement of every officer, every comment made by the Master to each and every officer he invested, and a dissertation on the delightful manner in which each address was delivered the vast majority of which was totally unnecessary to the occasion.

The secretary obviously had aspirations towards authorship and both this part of the proceedings and his deliberations on the risings which lasted some twenty minutes showed not only the folly of leaving a brother in office for far too many years but also the lack of control of the Master in cutting short such unnecessary rhetoric.

Let us now list those things which a set of minutes should contain.

First Brother Secretary should read Rule 144 and he will then see that there is a clear requirement to record the names of all persons initiated, passed and raised or becoming members together with their proposers and seconders, their ages, addresses, titles and professions or occupations.

Also required to be recorded are the names of every member and visitor present together with the name and number of the visiting brothers' lodges and also their masonic ranks.

Finally the rule continues, the minutes of all the proceedings of the lodge.

The important word here is proceedings, that means actual events not every movement, every word, action or gesture that occurs during a meeting.

It really is not necessary to set out here those things which should and should not be included, common sense will quickly indicate to Brother Secretary just how much can be omitted whilst still giving a comprehensive picture of the events which occurred during the meeting.

If you ever have a doubt whether or not to include something ask yourself this simple question.

Will the item which I am thinking of leaving out ever require to be substantiated in the future and is it vital to the requirements of Rule 144?

It should be possible for the minutes of a meeting to be incorporated in such a manner as to be contained on one sheet of A4 paper.

There is a current trend towards the photocopying of lodge minutes and circulating them with the next summons. This practice has the approval of the Grand Secretary and has two specific advantages.

First it saves a goodly portion of time during the meeting and secondly and perhaps even more importantly there is a far better chance of the brother receiving those minutes actually reading and digesting them.

Such a practice is used by this author in a senior lodge comprised almost exclusively of Grand Officers and the merits of this system cannot be too strongly recommended.

To assist those secretaries who may wish to take a totally new look at the art of writing minutes, an example of the brevity which can be effected is shown both for a normal meeting and the installation meeting.

THE INSTALLATION MEETING

Minutes of the xxxxxxx xxxxxxxxxxxxx Lodge No 0000 held at the Masonic Hall, St. John's Hill, Anytown, Wessex, on Monday 5th April 1999, commencing at 6.00.p.m.

The lodge was opened in due form and with solemn prayer in the three degrees by the Worshipful Master, x.x.x. xxxxxxxxxx, and resumed in the first degree.

The Worshipful Master rose to pay tribute to the life and work of W. Bro.x.x.x. xxxxxxxxxx, PAGDC, PProvSGW, and a Founder of this lodge. The brethren stood to order as a mark of respect to the memory of this departed brother.

The Minutes of the meeting held on Tuesday 2nd January 1999 having been circulated, were approved and signed by the Worshipful Master.

The lodge was resumed in the second degree. W. Bro. x.x.x. xxxxxxxxxx, was presented as Master-elect and duly recited his Obligation.

The lodge was resumed in the third degree and a Board of Installed Masters was then declared. W. Bro. x.x.x. xxxxxxxxxx, was duly Installed into the chair of King Solomon by the Worshipful Master x.x.x. xxxxxxxxxx.

The newly-installed Master was saluted in ancient form. The Board of Installed Masters was closed and the lodge was closed in the third and second degrees. Perambulations and salutations were given in each degree. The Worshipful Master duly invested his Officers, a list of which is attached to these Minutes.

The address to the Master was given by the W. Bro. x.x.x. xxxxxxx, to the Wardens by W. Bro. x.x.x. xxxxxxxxxx, and to the Brethren by W. Bro. x.x.x. xxxxxxxxxx.

Alms were collected which amounted to £200,00.

The Worshipful Master rose for the first, second, and third times. On the second rising the Treasurer announced that the fees for the ensuing year would remain unaltered at £75.00.

On the third rising the Secretary reported the resignation of W. Bro. x.x.x. xxxxxxxxxx. Apologies from nine brethren were read and recorded. There being nothing further for the good of Freemasonry the Lodge was closed at 7.30.p.m.

Date .... Worshipful Master

THE NORMAL MEETING

Minutes of the xxxxxxx xxxxxxxxxxxxxxx Lodge No. 0000 held at The Masonic Hall, St. John's Hill, Anytown, Wessex on Monday 2nd January 2000, commencing at 6.30.p.m.
The Lodge was opened in due form and with solemn prayer by the Worshipful Master xxxxxxxxx xxxxxx.

The Dispensation to hold the meeting on this date was read.

The Minutes of the meeting held on Monday 9th November 1999 having been circulated, these were approved and signed by the Worshipful Master.

The Accounts for the year ended 31st October 1999 were presented by the Treasurer. The auditors W. Bros xxxxxxx and xxxxxxxxx. confirmed their satisfaction. The accounts were then approved without dissent.

Pursuant to a Notice of Motion given on the 9th Nov 1999 the Secretary proposed and the Treasurer seconded 'That the September meeting be held on the First Tuesday in September and that By-Law No 1 be suitably amended'. This was approved.

Mr. A. B. Smith, a Candidate for Initiation, having been successfully balloted for at the meeting held on the 9th November 1999, was admitted and initiated into Freemasonry by the Worshipful Master in accordance with ancient custom. The charge was given by xxxxx.

A ballot for the Master for the ensuing year proved in favour of Bro. x.x.x. xxxxxxxxxxxxx.

A ballot for the Treasurer was in favour of W. Bro. x.x. xxxxxx.

On the proposal of W. Bro. xxxx xxx seconded by W. Bro. xxxx xxx W. Bro. xxx xxxxx was elected as Tyler by a show of hands.

W. Bros' x.x.x. xxxxxxx and x.x.x. xxxxxxx were elected as Auditors for the ensuing year. Proposed by W. Bro. xxx xxxxxx seconded by W. Bro. xxxxx xxxxxxxx.

Alms were collected in the sum of £150.00.

The Worshipful Master rose for the first, second and third times. Apologies for absence were received from six brethren whose names were duly recorded.

There being nothing further for the good of Freemasonry in general or this lodge in particular the lodge was closed at 7.49.p.m.

Date .... Worshipful Master

Chapter 21:

Passing or Raising a Candidate from Another Lodge

Rule 173 (a) states that '(a) No Lodge of which he is not a member shall pass or raise a Brother who has been initiated in another Lodge except at the written request of the Master (or in his absence a Warden) and the Secretary of the lodge in which he was initiated'.

This means in effect that providing proper permission has been given by the initiating lodge there is no reason at all why a brother cannot be passed or raised in another lodge of his choosing, and one which is prepared to carry out this ceremony.

It is of course the case that the work load of the initiating lodge is such that they would not be prepared to agree to such an action being taken in which case there is no more to be said.

However, it can sometimes be the case that a lodge has a large number of ceremonies building up and subject to the requirements of the lodge itself it may well be that it is the custom for only one ceremony to be carried out at any meeting of the lodge.

When such a circumstance prevails it can be of benefit for the lodge concerned to allow a ceremony to be performed by another which has little or no work to do, particularly if this should be a daughter lodge or a lodge with some other close association, meeting perhaps in the same venue.

Such thoughtful actions go a long way to create and cement relations between lodges, an action which is to be encouraged and fostered.

There are occasions when a brother from overseas is sent to this country for a period of years on a working assignment having taken his first degree in his home country, or that a brother has moved into the area from some distant part of the country.

Clearly to have to wait for a number of years before being passed and raised would impose an undue period of hardship on the brother so concerned and it is to be recommended, that where such a case exists, steps are taken to see that the situation is assisted to a natural conclusion. Do remember that permission has to be received in writing before your lodge can commence the process of progressing the brother further.

We now have to study Rule 173 (b) which deals with the passing and raising of a brother from another constitution.

The rules are slightly different but nevertheless if closely followed there should be no difficulty whatsoever in ensuring that progress to a satisfactory conclusion is ensured.

Where the converse obtains sub section (c) should be studied and enacted.

Whenever a Brother has been passed or raised under any of the provisions of this rule a document certifying such passing or raising shall forthwith be forwarded to the Grand Secretary and to the lodge to which the candidate belongs.

Chapter 22:

Candidates from Outside the Area

There can surely be few brethren who are not aware of the contents of Rule 158 of the Book of *Constitutions* and its application in regard to candidates from outside the catchment area of the masonic authority to which the lodge reports.

Clearly, as we will all know from our involvement and entry into the craft, it is frequently the case that upon showing interest in the order a prospective candidate will find he is talking to someone whose own masonic involvement is centred in another area.

This particularly applies in London with a border brushing against no less than five Provinces when the overspill factor comes very much into play as indeed it will on the borders of Provinces and Districts throughout the length and breadth of the Craft.

The purpose of this rule is to ensure that the masonic authority which has charge over the area in which the candidate either lives or works is made aware of the application to join a lodge outside their area of responsibility albeit he has neither living or working qualifications in the area of his application.

The majority of lodge secretaries will know that a simple enquiry to the appropriate masonic authority asking if they have knowledge of, and/or objection to the intended candidate for initiation, will produce a helpful and usually speedy reply.

Secretaries are advised that to read out a form of application before receiving such a clearance from another masonic authority is contrary to correct procedure and should not occur. It would also be unwise to conduct an interview of such a candidate until clearance is given.

Therefore, having received a form of application and recognising that it will require a clearance from another masonic authority, Brother Secretary must ensure that no plan is made to announce, read or otherwise proceed with the application before that clearance has been applied for and a positive response received.

Once received you may proceed with the normal method of processing the application for initiation.

The method of ascertaining the correct masonic authority to whom to apply is a simple matter of using the Masonic Year Book to advantage. If a borderline case is suspected then ring the Provincial Grand Secretary of the area in which you suspect the prospective candidate lives.

You will quickly get the right answer to your question and you can then send off your letter together with a stamped addressed envelope for the reply. Remember this courtesy, it helps.

Your letter should be simple in content. The following example may help the secretary who has never had to deal with this situation before.

To: Provincial Grand Secretary
Province of Somewhere,
100, High Street,
Anytown. CD22 0BB.   Date

Dear Sir and Brother,
        Mr Albert B. Anyone.
        1, Station Road,
        Anytown, AB11 0AB

This lodge has received an application for initiation from the above named gentleman who resides within the area of your masonic jurisdiction.

It would be appreciated if you would advise me if you have any knowledge of him and have any objection to this lodge proceeding with his application.

Your assistance would be appreciated.

Yours sincerely and fraternally,

J. Bloggs
Secretary.

Do please remember that the agreement of the Province or District to whom you apply is not automatic and there may well be an objection to the candidature of a particular person who might have applied to another lodge for admission and about whom the Province or District has kept a record.

Never assume that agreement to your proceeding with a candidate is a simple 'rubber stamping' operation. This may not be the case and both you and your lodge, to say nothing of the proposer and seconder, may have good reason to thank a well organised Provincial or District Secretary whose access to accurate records compiled and retained for many years may well save your lodge from such unhappiness which could be caused by proceeding with the candidature of an undesirable person.

Chapter 23:

The Register of Members

We read in Rule 146 (ii) that it is the 'duty' of every lodge to keep a record of all its members both past and present containing their dates of Initiation. Passing and Raising, or joining or rejoining, as the case may be, their ages, addresses, titles, and professions or occupations and the dates and reasons for their ceasing to be members.

The sensible and wise secretary will indeed keep a record of all of these things and allocate to each new member a full membership number in the register of members so kept. This should in turn lead to a comprehensive record card of the member concerned upon which should be recorded every office he holds in the lodge and the year in which he held it.

An example of such a card used in the author's lodge may be of assistance but the requirements of each lodge may well necessitate a unique card being produced to satisfy individual requirements.

The member's personal details such as his marital status, the christian names of his wife and children and their ages when the entry was made should be recorded, so that a clear and detailed picture can be ascertained from the register should an unforeseen circumstance befall the brother concerned and the lodge has to deal with a difficult situation at short notice.

The author had an occasion whilst secretary of his mother lodge to have to deal with correspondence from a relative of the widow of a brother who had been excluded from the lodge for non-payment of subscription some forty-four years previously.

Such was the record keeping of previous secretaries that this enquiry was dealt with in the minimum of time and with considerable accuracy.

Without such adequate records there would have been no chance at all of the enquiry being dealt with at local level and it would have had to have been referred to Grand Lodge whose records are of course not only of long standing but highly accurate.

Brother Almoner will also have good reason to thank a well organised secretary for when the lodge Almoner has a call upon his services this is most certainly not the time to try and find out the christian name of the wife of a member or a former member whose widow is in distress, or whether she has a family or not!

A comprehensive picture of details both personal and business will stand a zealous Secretary in good stead in the years which lie not only ahead of the brother concerned during his membership but for those years which follow his passing.

A well kept register can be a gold mine of information which can be kept until it is required, and even if it is not required how very comforting for the lodge to know that it has taken preventative action on behalf of its brethren in the event of such a need arising.

A copy of the application form used for the applicant's entry into the craft is an excellent starting point for the compilation of this information.

Name: .... Date of Birth: ....

Address: ....

....

....

....

....

....

Marital Status: .... Name of Wife: ....

Children: ....

....

....

Profession: ....

Tel No:

Home: .... Bus: ....

Date Application received: ....Date of Interview: ....

Date form read in lodge: .... Date of ballot: ....

Initiated: .... Passed: .... Raised: ....

Application form sent to Grand Lodge on: ....

Form giving details of Passing & Raising sent on: ....

Grand Lodge Certificate received: ....

Grand Lodge Certificate presented: ....

Year Offices held: Steward: .... I.G.: .... J.D.: ....

S.D.: .... J.W.: .... S.W.: .... W.M.: ....
Offices held since leaving the Master's chair.

....

....

Other Lodges of which a member: ....

....

....

PROMOTION DETAILS
LONDON GRAND RANK
Recommended by the Past Masters' at a meeting on: ....
Recommendation form sent to Grand Lodge for L.G.R.: ....
Letter of appointment received: ....
Invested: ....
Letter recommending appointment to S.L.G.R. sent on: ....
Reply received: ....
Letter of appointment received: ....
Invested on: ....
Letter recommending appointment to Grand Rank sent: ....
Reply received: ....
Appointed to: .... Invested on: ....
Promoted to: .... Invested on: ....

PROVINCIAL OR DISTRICT GRAND RANK.
Form received from the Province or District: ....
Form return on: ....
Appointed to: .... Invested on: ....
Promoted to: .... Invested on: ....
Promoted to: .... Invested on: ....
Letter recommending appointment to Grand Rank sent: ....
Reply received: ....
Appointed to: .... Invested on: ....
Promoted to: .... Invested on: ....
Date of Death: ....

Chapter 24:

The Postponement of the Installation Meeting

The very thought of having to postpone an Installation meeting with all the attendant unhappiness and rearranging which will be necessitated can dampen the enthusiasm of the most zealous member of the craft.

Sadly it does sometimes happen and knowing what to do in such a circumstance is essential, for you may be quite sure that the membership will, with one voice, turn to Brother Secretary with a plaintive cry of 'What do we do now?' when faced with such a situation.

Rule 108 in its three quite separate sections deals with the anomalies which can occur from a Master-elect being willing to accept the office but unable to be present, to the outgoing Master continuing in office for another year.

It further deals with a situation where a Board of Installed Masters cannot be formed because of lack of qualified brethren.

If there should be any particular problem which it is considered is not covered by Rule 108 an enquiry at the Provincial or District Office will enable a clear decision to be obtained.

Chapter 25:

The Visit of the Provincial or District Representative, or Visiting Grand Officer (in London)

In most if not all Provinces and Districts an annual visit is made to each lodge within its jurisdiction by that masonic authority.

In London in recent years a Visiting Grand Officer scheme has been introduced which allowed any lodge without its own Grand Officer to make application for such a visit.

The purpose of this chapter is to explain the procedure to be adopted when news of an official visitor is made known to Brother Secretary.

It will quite obviously be the wish of the members to show THEIR lodge in the best possible light to the visitor concerned.

Such a course of action should be commenced with a nicely phrased letter of welcome in which Brother Secretary should tell the distinguished visitor something of the history of the lodge, its formation, its membership, its activities and current aims in regard to charity.

The trend in membership will be one subject to interest your visitor as will attendance at meetings, donations to charity in recent years and the standing of membership applications awaiting processing.

In your letter you should ensure that precise details of your location are given together with a small map of the area if your visitor has not visited your meeting place before and even if he has it shows good standards of organisation.

You should tell him he will be met on arrival by (and then give a name) Bro . . . who will have reserved a car parking space for him (if this is applicable).

Upon being met the visitor should be taken to the Director of Ceremonies who will take charge of him and introduce him to the Master, Wardens, Secretary and Treasurer.

You should advise him in your letter of any small duty you wish him to carry out for you such as presenting a Grand Lodge Certificate, or closing the VSL at the end of the meeting.

You should tell him that on the day of the meeting the Director of Ceremonies will explain to him the manner in which this will occur so that he does not receive a surprise when such a presentation is announced.

Explain to your visitor the timings of the meeting so that he has a clear picture of the events of the day and can plan his arrival accordingly. Last and not least send to him a copy of the summons.

When your visitor arrives the Director of Ceremonies should ensure that the visitor is shown both his seat in the lodge and that the other events in which he is to participate are fully explained to him.

Make such arrangements as may be necessary to ensure that your distinguished visitor is supplied with suitable refreshment without delay in the period between the end of the meeting and the start of the social board. Always ensure he is attended and never left to find his own way around your meeting place.

If bar space is normally limited then alternative arrangements should be made so that the visitor can, with a given degree of comfort, meet the members of the lodge.

He will undoubtedly wish to elicit from the principal officers as much information about the lodge and its members as possible to enable him to give a clear report to his Provincial or District Grand Master or Grand Secretary as is applicable.

Entry into the social board would normally start with the announcement that the Master and his distinguished visitor were ready to enter.

There are occasions when a distinguished visitor will prefer to forgo this courtesy and be within the room to receive the Master particularly if this should be the night of his installation.

The point to be made here is that the visitor should be asked what he would prefer to do rather than be told by the Director of Ceremonies what will happen.

This is but a small courtesy but it will assist in showing the organisation which you have in place for such occasions.

At the appropriate place on the toast list the time will arrive for the visitor to reply to the toast to his Province or District or if in London then to Grand Officers present and past.

It is always appreciated and it is a courtesy when the Master gives a short speech of welcome to the visitor and then calls for the toast to be drunk rather than ignoring the visitor and just getting on with the toast list as normal.

The Director of Ceremonies should ensure that the visitor is announced correctly before he rises to speak and that his correct style and title is used as well as his masonic rank.

When the visitor is ready to leave your social board he should be escorted to his car by at least two of the senior members of the lodge and thanked for attending.

The message here is to treat others, particularly official visitors, as you yourself would wish to be treated.

The visitor probably knew nothing of your lodge prior to his visit so every scrap of digestible information forthcoming from you as secretary will be willingly accepted and will give to him a nicely rounded impression of you, your lodge and its organisation.

When the occasion of a visit by a Provincial Grand Master or his Deputy or Assistants takes place a wholly differing set of additional requirements come into play which will be explained by the Provincial Grand Director of Ceremonies or one of his Deputies attending upon such a dignitary.

Chapter 26:

Responsibility for the Lodge of Instruction

It is frequently the case that members of a Lodge of Instruction decide to take some action or other only to find they are reminded to their complete surprise that they do not possess the authority for making that decision.

Lodges of Instruction exist, not as is often thought under their own authority, but under the direct responsibility and control of the lodge itself.

The existence or otherwise of a Lodge of Instruction, its constitution, the minutes of its meetings and its place of abode are all decisions which have to be made by resolution of and taken within the lodge itself.

For the uninformed or newly appointed secretary Rules 132 to 135 of the Book of *Constitutions* deal with the formation, the behaviour and the actions of that Lodge of Instruction.

If a lodge which has given its sanction for a Lodge of Instruction being held shall see fit, it may at any regular meeting withdraw that sanction by a resolution of the lodge, provided that notice of intention to withdraw the sanction be inserted in the summons for that meeting, and at the same time be communicated to the secretary of the Lodge of Instruction.

A decision to withdraw the sanction for the holding of a Lodge of Instruction shall be notified to the secretary of the Lodge of Instruction which shall thereupon cease to exist.

The decision shall also be notified to the Grand Secretary or the Provincial or District Grand Secretary, as the case may be.

The reading of the two rules mentioned will assist Brother Secretary in any negotiations he may be required to hold with the membership of the Lodge of Instruction.

As always in such matters it is to be hoped that sensible consultations will prevail in any matters where disagreement occurs.

It is perhaps worth mentioning a few words at this juncture in regard to the often experienced 'tail wagging the dog' syndrome which can and frequently does occur in Lodges of Instruction.

It is often the case that because of the regular weekly meetings of the Lodge of Instruction, and also because the younger, and who can argue, the more enthusiastic members predominate at such meetings that the brethren so gathered believe that they 'are' the lodge and may well try to alter, change or otherwise adapt, amend or scrap, some well established procedure.

At times such as this the wisdom of Solomon indeed needs to prevail if the enthusiasm and energy of such members are not to be used unwisely or dissipated entirely.

Brother Secretary with his considerable knowledge of all the members, can often with considerable advantage talk to the membership and listen to their wishes with a considerate and helpful approach rather than in a defensive or, even worse, an aggressive posture.

All young masons like to flex their enthusiastic muscles occasionally and it is the manner in which such flexing is handled that makes for a secretary of stature and respect rather than a hard immovable 'know it all' type of individual.

The latter type of secretary will quickly become the last person to whom the brethren will turn for advice, and one who will be regarded as a martinet rather than the easily approachable individual which all good secretaries should be, and thereby loved for their approachability.

Remember that the Lodge of Instruction is where the step by step progress is made and we should never forget our own faltering attempts at the ritual and perhaps thereby understand and be sympathetic in all our dealings with younger brethren 'flexing their muscles'.

Chapter 27:

Minutes of the Lodge of Instruction

Rule 134 of the Book of *Constitutions* lays down quite clearly the requirement for the Lodge of Instruction to keep detailed minutes of its proceedings and record the names of those brethren who are present at each meeting as well as those who are appointed to hold office.

The minutes of any and every meeting held shall be as full as is necessary to present a composite picture of the events which occurred at that meeting.

Such minutes may be required to be inspected by the masonic authority responsible for the area to which the lodge, and thereby the Lodge of Instruction, reports.

It is usual for the Lodge of Instruction annually to elect a Preceptor to take charge of the teaching and training of the brethren attending.

A secretary and treasurer are two other annual appointments usually made.

Such appointments should be recorded in the minutes of the Lodge of Instruction so that accountability can be clearly elicited should such ever be needed.

It is said that the Lodge of Instruction is the heart of the lodge and few would deny that statement.

For this is where, week by week, the growing takes place and the lodge meeting becomes the place where the result of all that hard work is put on show.

A strong Lodge of Instruction usually begets a strong lodge and good work at the Lodge of Instruction usually results in a lodge where the standards are high and the reputation of the lodge is also of the highest order.

Chapter 28:

Clearance Certificates

A Lodge shall grant a Certificate free of charge to a Brother whenever required by him in each of the following cases: So starts Rule 175 of the Book of *Constitutions*.

What follows covers two quite different situations, the first of which deals with the requirement of a brother to prove he is not in debt to the lodge and that his dues for the current year are fully paid.

The second deals with the requirement of a former member who due to resignation from the lodge has ceased his membership but requires now to join another lodge and is in need of proof of his good standing with his former lodge.

If such a brother be under suspension such information should be included on any certificate issued.

Except as provided in this rule no other certificate of any kind may be issued by a lodge to any of its members.

In particular, a brother who has been expelled from the Craft under Rule 277A shall not be granted a certificate.

There are many reasons why a brother will require a certificate proving his good standing in the lodge of whom he is requesting such a certificate.

A brother seeking to be a founder of a new lodge will require to prove his good standing and will have to produce a certificate from each and every lodge of which he is or has been a member.

A brother removing to another country will require a certificate when he attempts to join a new lodge.

In the case of a Brother whose membership has ceased as a result of Rule 148 (non-payment of subscription for two years) or who has been the subject of a by-law covering a shorter period as outlined in Rule 181 such fact(s) should be recorded on the Clearance Certificate issued to the Brother concerned.

If subsequent to either of these actions occurring the outstanding subscriptions are paid then the fact shall be notified to the Grand

Secretary, and if the Lodge be within a Province or District, also to the Provincial or District Grand Secretary.

In the United States of America in particular it is essential that a visiting brother take substantive proof of his good standing in his lodge.

This author on a visit to Maryland visited a lodge in Baltimore and besides being proved in all three degrees also had to give proof of having paid his current year's subscription.

So be warned Brother Secretary and what is more warn your brethren that they will require such a certificate if they are travelling abroad and intend to visit a lodge in that foreign country. Without that certificate they could well be refused admission.

What exactly do we mean when we use the word 'certificate'? The simple answer is any form of declaration which states that:

'Brother . . . has been a member of this lodge since 19. . . and is free of all dues owing to this the . . . Lodge number . . .'

Any such certificate should be signed by either the lodge Treasurer or Secretary and in some lodges both.

Brother Secretary should however be quite sure if he is the producer of such a certificate that he has the confirmation of the Treasurer that the statement he is making is correct.

It should be said finally that no charge should be made for the supply of any of the certificates mentioned.

Chapter 29:

Death of the Master and Other Contingencies

What a shock it must be for any lodge to learn that their master has died.

After the first and immediate shock has passed what then are the rules which should be observed and which cover the consequent management of the lodge?

Inspection of Rule 119 of the Book of *Constitutions* will show the several and various actions which will require to be taken should the master of the lodge die during his year in office or indeed if he should for any reason be prevented from attending to his duties for the period of his mastership.

The meetings of the lodge shall be called by the Senior Warden or in his absence the Junior Warden or in the absence of both Wardens the Immediate Past Master or in his absence the senior Past Master of the lodge.

On occasions when the master is absent for just one meeting it is of course quite normal for the Immediate Past Master to take charge of the meeting.

Should he not be present then the senior Past Master present should officiate. End of Rule 119 (b).

It is interesting to note that if no Installed Master be present at a meeting of the lodge then that meeting shall be abandoned and the fact entered in the minute book of the lodge.

The full reading of this rule is recommended to Brother Secretary for it has the answers to a number of variations covered under the general heading of 'other contingencies'.

Fortunately the frequency of such a happening occurring in a lodge are rare but this very fact means that experience of the majority of secretaries in handling such a difficult situation is probably nil.

Let us ensure that we know what to do should such an occasion arise, but at the same time pray that we never have to use that knowledge to effect in our lodge.

Chapter 30:

Period Between the Conferring of Degrees

This subject is dealt with in two parts, for the details which apply vary according to the location of the lodge, the difference in timing between Provinces and Districts being considerable.

We shall therefore deal with each of these situations separately.

In Provinces no lodge shall confer a degree on any brother at a less interval than four weeks from his receiving the previous degree, and every ceremony performed in contravention of this provision shall be void.

Should any ceremony be performed in contravention of this rule such breach of Rule 172 shall be referred by the Grand Master to the Board of General Purposes but he may if he thinks proper upon a recommendation of the Board grant a dispensation validating any such ceremony retrospectively, subject to such (if any) conditions as he may consider proper.

In Districts, the District Grand Master may, under his own authority, given by dispensation, reduce the period between the conferring of degrees to not less than one week if he so decides.

Where a lodge is not under a District such authority must come from the Grand Master.

It is indeed most unlikely that any lodge would wish to organise its programme of work whereby it was found to be conferring a degree on a brother more frequently than once in four weeks.

One should always remember that the period of time allocated between each degree is for the benefit of the candidate, to enable him to learn a little of his new status in the lodge and the history and meaning of his role in the affairs of the lodge, to say nothing of his new station in Freemasonry.

Rushing any candidate through the three degrees of craft masonry is ill-advised and can lead to a situation whereby the candidate finds he has reached a plateau in a few short months and his potential appointment as a steward is still some five or six years ahead.

This is the period when you are very likely to find him missing a meeting here and there and generally toning down his involvement simply because there is nothing exciting to look forward to in the immediate future.

When the author became the founding secretary of a new lodge in 1972 the founders decided that a candidate after initiation should not be passed for at least twelve months and after passing he should not be raised for a further twelve months.

As you would expect this brought many plaintive appeals from newly initiated brethren who had seen friends made master masons in as short a time as three months.

The founders refused to alter their decision and surprisingly this author who was also the Preceptor of the Lodge of Instruction remembers well the many occasions when brethren came to him after waiting for their period of training in their new degree to pass, to say how much they realised with hindsight they had not been ready to take another degree twelve months earlier.

They appreciated that they had known nothing of the degree through which they had passed and had benefited considerably by being made to wait. They also said they then felt they had 'earned' their new rank, rather than simply having a different apron placed about their waist as a matter of course.

Remember that a sense of achievement is always felt when anything is earned rather than just being given without effort.

A goodly supply of psychology is required for any lodge to institute such a system but one thing is sure, you will retain the interest of the brother concerned and he will feel a sense of seniority when he is conducted through another degree, for it will be an outward sign to the other members of the length of his membership of the lodge.

It should always be remembered that candidates are not 'fodder' on which the lodge runs its meetings, they are prized new members and they should be shown great consideration and affection as well as a sense of being needed and necessary, particularly in their formative years in the lodge. They most certainly should never become just 'the candidate' for passing or raising at the next meeting.

It is all too easy for this to happen if great care is not taken of all newly made members of our order.

Chapter 31:

A Visit by the Provincial or District Grand Master or the Deputy or Assistant

The occasion of a visit from the Provincial or District Grand Master, their Deputies or Assistants is indeed an event of rare proportions.

Every detail of such a happening must of course be handled with the greatest possible care to ensure that not only is your lodge presented in the best possible light but also that the brethren of the lodge are instructed in every detail of the visit and the part which they will play in ensuring its success.

Such dignitaries will normally be accompanied by their own Director of Ceremonies who will undoubtedly make contact with you prior to the day of the meeting and will very probably wish to talk to the lodge Director of Ceremonies as well.

It is possible that you will be given a printed list of instructions of the major features of the visit including the entry and exit of the dignitary from the lodge.

There is no set pattern of timing for the entry of such VIPs each meeting being a total entity unto itself.

It is usual for the Director of Ceremonies accompanying the VIP to request admission and once inside the lodge DEMAND admission for his superior.

A procession of lodge officers is formed by the visiting Director of Ceremonies and this procession proceeds outside the door of the lodge to escort the dignitary into the temple.

Once inside the visitor will salute the Master and proceed to the East to be presented with the gavel. It is usual for him to return it with grateful thanks.

The Provincial or District Grand Director of Ceremonies will then instruct the escort to be seated as well as the brethren standing in the temple.

At this point the Provincial or District Grand Director of Ceremonies will call upon the brethren to salute the dignitary with the appropriate number of salutations for the rank of the visitor. For the record these are as follows:

Seven for a Provincial or District Grand Master being a Right Worshipful brother and thereby so entitled.
Five for a brother of Very Worshipful rank.
Five for a Deputy or Assistant Provincial or District Grand Master in their own Province or District but three elsewhere providing of course that they are Grand Officers and thereby so entitled.

The Book of *Constitutions* Rule 6 shows the precise details which apply in every situation.

The closing of the VSL will normally be undertaken by the visiting dignitary escorted of course by his own Director of Ceremonies.

The remainder of the meeting will usually be left to the team of officers of the lodge.

The lodge Director of Ceremonies will form the closing procession if one is so formed in your lodge and at the point of entry to that procession of the Provincial or District Grand Master his Deputy or Assistant, the Provincial or District Grand Director of Ceremonies will take over the remainder of the outgoing procession. Just occasionally the visiting dignitary will wish to leave the temple prior to the risings and the Provincial or District Grand Director of Ceremonies will take charge of its formation and departure.

During the period immediately after the closure of the lodge the visiting dignitary will undoubtedly wish to meet the brethren of the lodge including yourself as the lodge secretary and the brethren should be advised in advance to be ready to be called, particularly if they are in office.

It is the custom, and in most cases the practice, for the visiting dignitary to speak to the Charity Steward the Immediate Past Master (if there has been an Installation) and Treasurer of the lodge to say nothing of the Director of Ceremonies and any other officer who has perhaps performed some role in the foregoing proceedings.

Elderly Past Masters are frequently left out of such an occasion. It is however important that the older and more senior brethren are introduced for a brief period to the visitor and a little of their service to the lodge explained.

This is not the time for visitors to be introduced for the visiting dignitary for it is of the lodge and its members that he wishes to get an impression not the brethren who are visiting the lodge.

The Social Board will bring yet a further addition to the normal proceedings for the Provincial or District Grand Master, the Deputy or Assistant, will reply to their own toast and it is always an extremely good idea for the Master to make a special point of giving a short but welcoming speech before calling upon the brethren to honour the toast he is proposing.

The reply to the toast will be announced by the Provincial or District Grand Director of Ceremonies who will then call for silence whilst the reply is delivered.

It is not unusual for the visiting dignitary to retire from the social board a little before its conclusion and the Provincial or District Grand Director of Ceremonies will call for the brethren to stand whilst the VIP retires from the room.

It is always a polite and most acceptable gesture for a small party of say two or three senior members to retire at the same time and thank the visitor for coming to the lodge on this occasion and then see him to his car or transport.

A letter of thanks from Brother Secretary a day or so after the meeting is also a polite and courteous action to take.

Any individual is subject to impressions about anything, we all know the first impression we have of a place we have never been to before, a person we meet for the first time, the new home of a friend. Why then should we assume that our visitor is any different from us. He too will be equally as impressed or disillusioned with what he sees, with what he hears, and also what he experiences.

The last is the most difficult to handle whilst the first two are both within the organising capability of the Director of Ceremonies and Secretary and should be considered carefully before a visit takes place.

These visits take place very infrequently and should be handled with great care for the impression thus gained of your lodge will remain with that dignitary for a very long time to come, possibly for the duration of his Provincial or District Grand Mastership.

Chapter 32:

The Consecration of a Lodge

The Consecration is of course the single most important event which can occur in the lifetime of a lodge for it brings into being an entity which had previously not existed.

The ceremony itself contains a number of essential elements which as far as can be confirmed have been present since the official consecrating of lodges began.

It may come as a surprise to the reader to learn that the official act of Consecration (followed by the first regular meeting of the lodge) as now practised is a relatively new procedure, though 'The Antient Manner of Constituting a Lodge' was detailed in the 1738 edition of Anderson's Book of Constitutions.

Prior to this a new lodge would simply be granted a Warrant and start holding meetings without, as far as can be ascertained, any official ceremony whatsoever before beginning its new life.

It is difficult to date precisely the first known ceremony of Consecration. However what is known from established records is that since the union of the two Grand Lodges in 1813 there has been a requirement for the Grand Master or someone designated by him 'solemnly' to constitute every new lodge.

In these days that task is carried out by the Provincial or District Grand Master for those areas outside London and frequently by the Grand Secretary for new lodges formed within the London area.

The general administration of lodges, their organisation into groups of Provinces or Districts has improved beyond all measure from that which existed prior to the Union.

What then can Brother Secretary designate do to ensure that this important event in the life of the lodge remains a day to remember both for those who participate as well as those who simply come to watch and support.

Let us start with the application to the masonic authority responsible for the area in which the new lodge is scheduled to meet.

A letter to the Grand Secretary in the case of London or the Provincial or District Grand Secretary will usually receive a response inviting the Master and Wardens designate to a meeting. At this meeting the general features of the formation of a new lodge will be discussed and many questions will be asked and (we hope) answered to the satisfaction of that official.

Assuming that all progresses well, another meeting may well be scheduled at which the Deputy or Assistant Provincial or District Grand Master will call for a meeting with all the Petitioners (the name given to the Founders prior to the Consecration).

It is essential that at this meeting the answers which will be given to the questions that undoubtedly will be asked have been carefully considered and that a clear and well formulated reason for the formation of the lodge is put forth.

Providing that this meeting is satisfactory to the management of the Province or District, then the Provincial or District Grand Master will probably give his assent to the issue of a Petition for completion and subsequent forwarding to Grand Lodge for approval.

The form for completion by the Petitioners will require to have attached to it clearance certificates for every petitioner from every lodge of which he is, or has been a member.

This can be a lengthy business for some petitioners who may well belong to many lodges perhaps even some of whom are overseas. It should be mentioned at this time that six to eight weeks is not an unusual period for this task to be accomplished.

The form being completed and the clearance certificates being to hand, this should be returned to the masonic authority that issued it. Great care must be taken in the completion of this form for unless it is completely accurate in every particular it will mean a delay whilst such matters are corrected.

This will, after being checked, be forwarded to Grand Lodge for them to check that each signature is valid and that the details of each Petitioner are as they have them so recorded in their records.

Eventually the Provincial or District Grand Secretary will receive notice of the satisfaction of Grand Lodge and agreement to the name of the new lodge.

At this point a lodge number will be allocated.

The Province or District will, after consultation, advise a date for the Consecration which in turn will be communicated to the Petitioners.

You now have a firm date for your diary, a date to which everyone concerned with the formation of this new lodge can plan and concentrate their organisation.

Ensure that this date is known to everyone involved immediately you know of it.

Close planning with the masonic authority well in advance of the occasion is essential.

A list of who does what, when, and in some cases how, is essential if every facet of the day is to pass without problem on what will surely be the 'big day' in the life of the lodge namely its 'birthday'.

There are many things which will require your attention before that day arrives.

Doubtless many meetings of the Petitioners will occur and it is the fine planning which should be organised at such meetings.

Assuming that such decisions regarding the venue for the meetings, the dates of the meetings, and the designated officers have been decided, let us examine some (not all by any means) of the items which will require the involvement of Brother Secretary-designate prior to the day of the Consecration.

It is probable that many of the things which require to be done will require to be delegated to various brethren of the proposed new lodge.

A simple example is set out hereunder:

1. Where will the Consecration take place?
2. How many can the temple hold?
3. How many do we expect to attend?
4. What will be the the number of the Consecration team?
5. Catering — Cost?
   When are final numbers required?
   Precise detail of menu for the brochure?
   Timing?
   Tea prior to the meeting?
   Refreshments for the Consecration team both before and after the meeting?
6. Printing of applications for tickets and dining?
7. Printing of brochures — required by date?
8. Printing of Invitation tickets — required by date?
9. When are they being sent out?
10. When do you require the replies back?
11. Founders' Fees — required by date?

12. Provision of Regalia and/or lodge furniture?
13. Founders' Jewels?
14. Cost of Warrant?
15. Provincial or District costs?
16. Presentation to the Consecrating Officer?
17. Secretarial requirements — books — forms etc?
18. When are final numbers of guests required from the Petitioners?
19. Rehearsal date fixed by the Consecrating Director of Ceremonies?
20. Changing room accommodation for V.I.Ps?
21. Car parking for V.I.Ps?
22. Starting and finishing times?
23. Ticketing of seats?
24. Timing for all the events noted?
25. Is the lodge well structured financially?
26. Letters of appreciation after the Consecration to?

>Consecrating Officer.
>Provincial or District Office.
>Caterer.
>Provincial or District D.C.
>Anyone else who assisted.

Although it may sound unnecessary to say so it really is most important that the administration of a new lodge is placed under the care of an experienced lodge secretary.

The form and content of minutes and the information they contain which begin the life of the lodge is very often recorded in almost the same format fifty years later. Brother Secretary will be well-advised to refer back to Chapter 20 for suggestions regarding this matter.

Secretaries who follow the first appointee to that office in the lodge will usually out of courtesy tend to use precisely the same layout and phrases as were used by their predecessors. It is therefore wise to ensure that we commence the records in a structured and well organised way.

Finally as the Consecration of a lodge may well be a new experience to the majority if not all of its petitioners, this can well be the period of consolidation of brother working with brother for the first time.

The teamwork which can and should ensue from the bringing into life of a totally new entity can build and mould a strong and cohesive team of brethren into a real lodge of members united in their single minded aim of spreading Freemasonry to a wider audience.

Whilst not failing to maintain the solemnity of the occasion, never forget that there should always be an element of fun in the hard work and indeed everything that we undertake and this applies no less to the Consecration of a new lodge than any other masonic activity.

Chapter 33:

Resignation from the Lodge

If we read Rule 183 we find that the detail connected with the resignation of a brother has a variety of applications.

A brother may if he so wishes resign with immediate effect. He may resign from a date in the future specified by him. He may resign either in writing to the lodge secretary or orally in open lodge.

What then should Brother Secretary do when he receives such a resignation?

They usually occur under three distinct headings. Firstly because of old age, infirmity, moving from the area or permanent inability to attend meetings, or an inability to meet the financial obligations in regard to annual subscriptions.

Secondly, from a disillusionment with his involvement with the lodge or perhaps its membership.

Thirdly, from a disagreement with a brother or a policy decision of the lodge which he finds he cannot accept.

Let us examine the subject of resignation in its widest intention.

To resign from anything is to express a wish to cease to have a further relationship be that a paid employment, membership of any organisation, to leave an honorary post, or to cease payment for a service received.

Resignation from a lodge is looked upon by many brethren as an action bringing with it some sense of shame. Such however should certainly not be the case.

To resign from a lodge having paid such subscriptions which are due is an honourable and decent action to take and is to be thoroughly recommended rather than allowing annual dues to mount up until the time arrives for the brother concerned to be excluded with the subsequent notation against his name in the registers of Grand Lodge.

What then should Brother Secretary do when he receives a letter of resignation from a brother?

Clearly he will, as the centre pin of the lodge activities, know under which heading this resignation has been written.

Should it be for any of the reasons given under the first grouping above there will only remain the duty of reading this out to the lodge on the appropriate rising at the next lodge meeting.

Should the resignation fall under categories two or three there may be a good reason for a meeting with the brother so concerned to see whether or not this is the best course of action to take, and whether the action is irrevocable, or if in fact some form of regeneration of interest or reconciliation can be arranged.

The decision to resign or not to resign is entirely that of the brother so concerned and his wishes must at all times be paramount. Brother Secretary none the less has a duty to ensure that he fully appreciates all that resignation from the lodge will mean.

To lose a brother by resignation is always sad but we have to be realistic in admitting that brethren do lose interest and do have personal disagreements with other brethren.

Freemasonry is after all composed of a cross section of humanity with all its attendant vagaries.

Resignations should be noted and communicated both to the Province or District and to Grand Lodge when the next occasion arrives for the completion of the annual return to any of them.

Such details as are appropriate should be included in the installation return if applicable.

The brother so resigning must be made aware of his indebtedness to the lodge in relationship to his Grand Lodge dues and his Provincial or District Grand Lodge dues.

Brother Secretary is under a duty not to allow a brother to disappear or cease his masonic involvement with the lodge without first advising such brother of his outstanding financial obligation and thereby be included as having left the lodge or the craft owing monies.

There may well be an occasion in the future when such brother wishes to join another lodge and will require a clearance certificate showing his freedom from outstanding dept upon his leaving the lodge.

It is also worth mentioning here that he is entitled to a clearance certificate if he asks for such when he has resigned providing of course that he is clear of all debt to the lodge upon his resignation taking effect.

Chapter 34:

Grand Rank

There can scarcely be a more emotive subject than that concerning the awarding or not awarding of Grand Rank.

In recent times the whole subject of candidature for Grand Rank has been clarified by the Grand Secretary and helpful literature is available from the United Grand Lodge of England to those who apply.

In simple terms the following information will direct recommendations to the authority responsible for forwarding such names to Grand Lodge.

Every brother recommended must be a Past Master of a lodge operating under the United Grand Lodge of England.

In Provinces and Districts all recommendations for Grand Rank are at the hand of the Provincial or District Grand Master who has a regular annual allocation of recommendation forms to complete.

This is not in itself a guarantee that a name thus recommended will automatically be granted that honour, but in the majority of cases the name put forward usually receives that honour which has been requested.

All recommendations from lodges within Provinces or Districts should be directed to the Provincial or District Grand Master via the Provincial or District Grand Secretary for that masonic authority.

In London any lodge may place before the Grand Secretary the name of a suitably qualified Past Master whom the Past Masters of the lodge consider to be worthy of such an honour.

The fullest details should be given of the brother thus recommended including the full details of his masonic involvement, the names and numbers of all his lodges and chapters, those lodges and chapters of which he has been a Founder, his periods of office in the several and various offices within the lodges and chapters of which he is or has been a member, and such general attributes which set him apart from others in qualification for consideration for such an honour.

Once this application or recommendation has been made no further or subsequent name will be accepted from that lodge until either the brother so named has been withdrawn or a grant of Grand Rank has been made to the brother thus recommended.

It is usually the case that letters offering appointment to active or past rank are sent out by the Grand Secretary during the early part of March.

The Annual Investiture of those appointed to Grand Rank takes place (Rule 12) on the Wednesday next following St George's Day (23rd April) with the Annual Investiture of Supreme Grand Chapter Officers taking place the following day.

Promotion within Grand Rank is not as rare as one might imagine. A brother holding Grand Rank for a number of years, usually upwards of seven can be promoted upon recommendation of his lodge if in London and if approved by the Grand Master.

In Provinces or Districts a similar system applies in that each Provincial or District Grand Master is given the opportunity each year to recommend a predetermined number of brethren for consideration for promotion each year.

Once again such recommendations must receive the approval of the Grand Master but in practice it is rare for such a request to be refused.

As an aid to assisting Brother Secretary in formalising his thoughts regarding the requirements for such an honour prior to submitting an application the following points may be of help.

Every lodge has at least one brother who is outstanding in his involvement in the craft in effort, ability and dedication. Such brethren usually become a focal point within a lodge and are almost always self-recommending.

It does sometimes happen that when the subject of a recommendation for Grand Rank is entered upon there may well be two or more brethren who believe that their service, their seniority or one of another dozen reasons are *prima facie* cases why their name, rather than another brother's should be that which is submitted. Such situations are full of potential for unhappiness and disharmony.

If such a situation should prevail in your lodge the following suggestion for overcoming such potential implications for argument and heated discussion may assist.

First ask the Master who is in all probability far too junior in years of service to have a vested interest in the matter to submit the two names on a sheet of paper to all the Past Masters asking them to return to him privately, that sheet of paper with only one name recommended.

When he has those returns to hand the recommendation letter can then be prepared in the name of the brother so recommended and despatched to the Grand Secretary or the Provincial or District Grand Secretary for their attention.

A brother thus recommended must be under seventy years of age and it is suggested that of two applications on behalf of brethren of equal capability the brother aged between fifty to sixty is more likely to have success than the older brother.

It should be remembered that appointment to Grand Rank is made with the view not only of recognising the contribution that a brother has already made but the extra effort and period of service he will be able to give to the craft after he receives such an appointment.

Enquiries regarding the possible appointment or progression of an application for Grand Rank will NOT be entered into by the Grand Secretary's office, such decisions being the sole prerogative of the Grand Master and his advisers.

An application therefore remains on record until it is either granted or withdrawn.

Grand Officers once appointed will receive a personal copy of the Quarterly Communications from the date of their appointment onwards as well as the opportunity of becoming members of the Grand Officers' Mess.

In addition, a personal copy of the Grand Secretary's newsletter will be sent to each Grand Officer usually a week to ten days after each quarterly communication.

Chapter 35:

London Grand Rank and Provincial or District Grand Rank

Appointment to London Grand Rank is made by the decision of the Grand Master and his advisors.

Recommendations for this rank are made by means of an application form which is sent to London lodges by the Grand Secretary approximately one every two years. Until a brother who has been recommended has been successful in being granted that rank another form will not be issued. In practice there will always be an application form with either the lodge Secretary for completion, or with the Grand Secretary for consideration for appointment.

Lodges may occasionally have to decide whether a recommendation which has been made and not granted after say five years should in fact be withdrawn and another name submitted in place of the original person so recommended. This action if taken will undoubtedly cause much unhappiness to the brother whose name has to be withdrawn and the past masters of lodges bear a heavy responsibility when making their selection originally.

Lodges are advised most strongly NOT to use what is euphemistically called 'Buggins Turn' in other words the next name on the list of past masters of the lodge. Much thought should be given to the qualities of the person being so recommended not only for what he has already achieved but for what he will be able to give to the lodge in the years which lie ahead.

Lodges who think their recommendations through most carefully are far more likely to be successful in achieving a 'first year' appointment than those who use the 'Buggins Turn' system and whose selections lie for years without success simply because candidates with better qualifications are selected ahead of them. Once the original application has been acknowledged by the Grand Secretary, it should be kept up to date if the details vary. The recommendation will be considered by the Grand Master's advisers every year until it succeeds or is withdrawn. The decision regarding the leaving or withdrawing of an application already made is a matter for the Past Masters' of the lodge and no one else.

Recommendations for appointment to Senior London Grand Rank can be made directly to the Grand Secretary at Freemasons' Hall at any time on behalf of brethren who have served a minium of five years as a Holder of London Grand Rank.

When this new rank was instituted the selection of candidates for this honour was made from the records of such Holders of London Grand Rank held at Freemasons' Hall but time has necessitated a wider selection base created due in part to the very nature of London masonry.

It should be added here that any candidate so put forward must be of the highest possible calibre for there is always the outside possibility that a particularly talented brother may in fact be elevated to Grand Rank as a result of such a recommendation.

The appointment of Provincial or District Grand Officers is entirely at the hand of the Provincial or District Grand Master.

In Rule 60 and 68(a) Book of *Constitutions* (the former dealing with London the latter with Provinces and Districts) a schedule of the appointments allowed is set out for the information of the reader. The number of lodges operating within the Province or District determines the number of appointments to active rank, whereas the number of appointments to past rank are determined by an aggregate of not more than four appointments (both active and past) for every five lodges within the Province or District.

Promotions to any rank up to Past Provincial or District Senior Grand Warden, but not above, are not limited and the Provincial or District Grand Master may promote such worthy brethren as he considers merit such advancement.

Rule 73 states that no brother shall be appointed to either the office of Provincial or District Senior or Junior Grand Warden be that an active or past rank, unless he shall be a Master or a Past Master of a lodge.

It is usual for a newly appointed Provincial or District Grand Master to be allowed a special allocation of Past Provincial or District appointments to mark the start of his period of office.

The granting of this special allocation is covered under Rule 68 (b).

Chapter 36:

Resignation from the Craft

Until the late nineteen-eighties resignation from the craft was impossible for there existed no system by which a brother could do so no matter how much he might have wished for that facility.

A brother ceasing his membership of all the lodges of which he was a member simply became an unattached brother but a brother none the less he remained.

Rule 277A (a) has been created to allow the facility of resignation for brethren whose conduct is considered to be incompatible with membership of the craft.

The creation of this new rule has been brought about by the requirement to deal with the times in which we live and, sad to say, the behaviour of a very small proportion of the membership who are unable to live by the tenets which they have been taught.

It will be an unfortunate secretary who has reason to take any part in, or have a member who wishes to take part in, such an action but it would be wrong to omit the subject from such an all purpose book of advice to Brother Secretary as this.

Chapter 37:

Responsibility for Fees for Initiation or Joining

Rule 171 of the Book of *Constitutions* is a short but totally clear instruction. It states that any member who proposes or seconds a candidate for initiation or joining shall be responsible to the lodge for all fees payable under its by-laws in respect of such candidate.

Such a rule may perhaps come as a shock to the reader but in fact it should be known and appreciated by all members of the craft who have taken the time to read the Book of *Constitutions* from cover to cover!

In reality what usually occurs is that the proposer and seconder advise a prospective candidate of his financial obligation to the lodge in terms of the total amount involved and also tell him that such fees are payable either before or on the day of his initiation or joining.

Should such circumstances occur whereby the candidate does not remit his indebtedness to the lodge then the lodge Treasurer is acting within his elected office in calling for such sums to be paid by the candidate's proposer and seconder.

It is quite surprising just how many proposers and seconders have no idea of their responsibility in this matter.

Chapter 38:

Non-payment of Annual Subscriptions

Two rules namely 147 and 148 deal very clearly with the non-payment of annual subscriptions.

The former deals with the payment of annual dues to Grand Lodge and the financial indebtedness of any member whose subscription is not fully paid to his lodge.

The latter rule deals with the action which MUST be taken by the lodge when a member's subscriptions to his lodge remain unpaid for two full years.

This is not a rule which allows for interpretation by Brother Secretary, Brother Treasurer or anyone else. It is an instruction of the action which has to be taken once the two year period is reached and passed.

Members who through their own non-payment of subscriptions become deprived of their membership can only become members once again when their indebtedness is fully met to the lodge or lodges of which they were formally members.

They must then submit to the recognised procedure of being proposed and seconded once again if they wish to regain their former membership of that lodge.

Where such an instance as described in the previous paragraph take place it should be remembered that a former Past Master of the lodge will, upon rejoining, become the most junior Past Master of the lodge.

If the By-Laws of the lodge so provide, it is possible for the lodge to take action earlier under Rule 181.

Chapter 39:

Brethren Joining from Another Constitution

Rule 163 (e) of the Book of *Constitutions* deals with this subject in ample form but for the benefit of Brother Secretary to whom no doubt enquiries will be passed, let us examine a set of hypothetical but potential circumstances as they develop.

It is often the case that a brother who has been initiated in another Constitution will visit a lodge as a guest of one of the members of a different Constitution, or alternatively he could well be a visitor from overseas sent to your lodge by Grand Lodge in response to a request from that brother to visit a lodge in this Constitution.

After his visit, or perhaps visits, the brother may feel he has established a new home for his Freemasonry and ask to be allowed to return to future meetings. As a result of these visits a time may well arrive when the brother feels he would like to make his newly-formed friendship into a more permanent and contributory relationship.

Until this time the brother will of course have been wearing the regalia and probably using the signs of the Constitution under which he was initiated, which is perfectly in order. What then must happen when the brother expresses a wish of permanent membership?

Let us assume for the purpose of this explanation that there are brethren willing to propose and second him as a joining member and he duly completes the form used by all who wish to become members of our order or joining members from another Constitution.

You Brother Secretary, should apply to Grand Lodge if your own lodge be a London lodge and to the Provincial or District Grand Secretary if your lodge comes under that masonic jurisdiction, to confirm that the Grand Lodge under which the brother was initiated is recognized by our Grand Lodge. This is a requirement of the Rule, but if this enquiry was made before admitting the brother into the lodge on the first occasion, the reply may be taken as holding, unless the Secretary has news that recognition has been withdrawn.

Assuming that the response to your enquiry is satisfactory you may proceed in the usual manner with the preparations for the balloting and subject to a positive vote, his subsequent welcome into the lodge.

Rule 163 (f) states that within one year of his becoming a member of the lodge he shall make a declaration of obedience in open lodge to the Grand Master and signify his support of the rules and regulations of the United Grand Lodge of England.

In fact it is usually the case that he will perform this act of declaration to the new Constitution he has joined on the evening of his acceptance as a member.

He should from this night on and hereafter wear the regalia stipulated by the United Grand Lodge of England when in a lodge operating under its authority, whether as a member or visitor. A brother from another Constitution must not wear a Past Masters' Collar until this has been 'earned' as a result of his having been installed in the Master's chair of an English Constitution lodge.

It is a stipulation of this Rule sub-section (h) that every brother joining in this manner shall be presented with a copy of the Book of *Constitutions* of the United Grand Lodge of England. The Master will of course give him a copy of the lodge by-laws.

A lodge may enact in its by-laws that a candidate shall in addition to his joining fees pay such registration fees as are payable to Grand Lodge and, if applicable, to Provincial or District Grand Lodge.

Where this action is undertaken the candidate shall be informed BEFORE he becomes a member, of the fees thus accrued and the total amount due by him both to the lodge, Grand Lodge and Provincial or District Grand Lodge.

The signed declaration made by the newly-joined brother should be retained in the minute book of the lodge for future confirmation that the brother concerned was correctly admitted into our Constitution and that the rules of the United Grand Lodge of England were properly carried out.

Finally, do remember that a brother from another Constitution will in all probability have been taught signs for the degrees which are different from our own and until he joins the English Constitution he may practice that which he has been taught whilst he attends our Lodge.

When however he becomes a member of a lodge working under the jurisdiction of the United Grand Lodge of England he must of course alter his signs to those of the newly joined Constitution and thus be in conformity with the working used by his new lodge.

One of the great joys of our order is that whilst having differences in our workings we can at one and the same time be totally as one in all that we endeavour to achieve.

A brother joining from another Constitution may well be a source of much information and instruction and, in telling of his experiences and the customs in his own Constitutions may well broaden our horizons as well as our knowledge in masonic matters generally.

Chapter 40:
The Wearing of Masonic Jewels in the Lodge

The inclusion of this chapter is for the sole purpose of ensuring that often misquoted opinions on the wearing of masonic jewels can be corrected for the benefit of Brother Secretary.

The wearing of a Royal Arch breast jewel is allowed in a craft lodge be it that of a Companion, Principal, Holder of London, Provincial or District Grand Rank or Supreme Grand Chapter.

Where, one is sometimes asked, is it stated in the Book of *Constitutions* that the wearing of this jewel is allowed?

To answer this question one should return to the preamble given just before rule number 1 in the Book of *Constitutions* from which the following quote is taken 'Antient Masonry consists of three degrees and no more, viz., those of Entered Apprentice, the Fellow Craft, and the Master Mason, including the Supreme Order of the Holy Royal Arch'.

If one reads Rule 241 it will be seen the authority therein given under reference to 'pure Antient Masonry'. This then is the answer to the question 'Where does it say in the Book of *Constitutions* that we can wear a Royal Arch jewel in a Craft lodge?'

It should perhaps be mentioned here that there is reference to the subject in the small blue booklet entitled 'Information for the Guidance of members of the Craft' where in answer to the question 'May Royal Arch regalia be worn in a Craft Lodge?' the answer given is 'No; but approved Royal Arch Jewels may be worn suspended by ribbons of the appropriate colour.'

There are occasions when a breast jewel issued for the stewardship of an institution is declared a permanent jewel by the Grand Master and may thereafter be worn at the decision of the person to whom the jewel was awarded but by no one else.

Charity jewels and the wearing of them is dealt with in extension under Rule 253 sub sections (a) to (g).

Centenary Jewels and Bicentenary Jewels are worn as a result of the authority conferred by the granting of a Centenary or Bicentenary Warrant the sole purpose of which is to acknowledge the existence of the lodge or chapter so noted for a period of one hundred or two hundred years respectively.

Apart from those acknowledged jewels as outlined in the Book of *Constitutions* the wearing of jewels of other orders is not sanctioned. Finally, it is quite wrong for any jewel whatsoever to be worn appended to a collar other than a jewel of office or of rank of the wearer which would of course be attached to the point of that collar.

Chapter 41:

Continuance in Office of The Master

There are occasions albeit rare when the Master of a lodge finds he is required to serve a second year in office. This can be due to any of the reasons set out in Rule 107 where his duly elected successor is unable to accept the office to which he has been elected.

There are also occasions where the lodge itself wishes a master to serve another year in office. In either circumstances this will clearly bring into being a different set of circumstances from that normally experienced by a lodge at its installation meeting.

The following paragraphs may be of assistance to those who have little or no experience of the procedure which can or should be adopted or adapted to cover such a situation.

When the appropriate item is reached on the agenda the Director of Ceremonies should rise from his seat and standing in the South-east make ONE of the two following statements:

"Brethren, the duly elected Master for the ensuing year being unable to undertake his office, I proclaim that W. Bro... will continue in office as Master of the .... (state name and number) lodge for the ensuing year and I call upon you to salute him as Entered Apprentice Freemasons five times taking the time from me"

"Brethren W. Bro... having been duly elected as Worshipful Master of this lodge for the ensuing year I now proclaim him Worshipful Master of the .... (state name and number) lodge and I call upon you to salute him as Entered Apprentice Freemasons five times taking the time from me".

After this has been completed and the brethren are told to be seated the Director of Ceremonies then moves to the investiture of the Officers without further instruction. He moves to the centre of the lodge and says 'Worshipful Master, whom do you appoint your Senior Warden?' He then moves through the list of Officers and completes the meeting in the usual way.

It is quite unnecessary for the address to the Master to be given on this occasion. This also applies to the address to the Wardens if they are to continue in office for second year.

The address to the brethren should always be given.

The Secretary and Director of Ceremonies should remember that the adoption of either of these procedures will necessarily result in a very short meeting since none of the usual perambulations, salutations, or opening in any degree other than the first will take place.

The Secretary and Director of Ceremonies will require to plan the timing of such a meeting very carefully for the announcements and ceremonial described above will take only twenty to twenty-five minutes at the most.

It should be remembered that the Master of a lodge does not become entitled to a Past Masters' jewel until after his successor has been installed.

Chapter 42:

Co-operation with the Director of Ceremonies

The happy and successful operation of a lodge in all its many facets depends almost entirely upon the co-operation of all the officers working together in a cohesive team to produce meetings of quality, accuracy and happiness as well as giving considerable satisfaction to those who participate as well as those who watch.

The co-operation between Brother Secretary and Brother Director of Ceremonies is of all the possible combinations the most important to the successful operation of the lodge, particularly during the preparation and holding of its meetings.

A clear distinction between the areas of responsibility of administration and ceremonial is for the most part obvious to all but there are areas in the operation of both offices which can tend to blur the edges and where each officer needs the co-operation of the other if the meeting is to be trouble free.

It is therefore essential that a given amount of licence in the operation of both their offices is shown by each of these senior officers in the lodge.

A short conversation, by telephone if necessary, to discuss the various points which will make for a smooth meeting can go a very long way towards avoiding any problems.

The Director of Ceremonies will need to know of any important visitors who may be attending and their names and ranks and if they are Grand Officers in order that they may not only be properly seated but also correctly saluted at the appropriate stage in the proceedings.

If a candidate for initiation has invited guests, their names must also be advised to the Director of Ceremonies so that appropriate arrangements can be made not only for their reception but also for their seating in the lodge room.

The Director of Ceremonies will appreciate being told well in advance of the name or names of any officers who may not be attending in order that he can make suitable arrangements for a replacement to be advised and instructed (if necessary) in their temporary duties.

The organisation of the seating in the lodge is the responsibility of the Director of Ceremonies.

As with most things which can be arranged in advance he will be helped to no small degree by any assistance that Brother Secretary can give to him in advising him of the size of the attendance at any meeting so that he can provide seating for all who attend.

The early attendance on the part of both Brother Secretary and Brother Director of Ceremonies on the day of the meeting will assist materially the harmonious working relationship between these two officers.

It will give them time to discuss the finer points of the meeting and ensure they both have a total grasp of all that is to occur during the afternoon and evening as well as to clear any small point either of them felt could be a problem.

Where Brother Secretary requires the Director of Ceremonies to make a proposal or to second a motion he should ensure that this is agreed before the meeting commences so that the smooth operation of the administration and ceremonial of the lodge can be seen as efficient to all present.

Where there is any lack of co-operation between these two very important officers it is quickly sensed and noticed by the brethren and as a consequence the lodge will suffer by being seen to be unsure of its programme for the meeting.

Chapter 43:

Election of an Honorary Member from Another Constitution

There would appear to be no rule at all governing the election of a brother from another Constitution to honorary membership of a lodge.

Sensibly it would appear to be such a rare occurrence that the passing of a rule for such a situation was considered unnecessary.

If one reads Rule 167 carefully it can be seen that the clear instruction given therein deals with brethren who have rendered specific and useful service to the lodge and does not necessarily refer to brethren of the Constitution of the United Grand Lodge of England.

In such a case it is reasonable to assume that the rule covers 'Freemasons' not just those operating under the Rules and Constitutions of the United Grand Lodge of England.

Perhaps a proviso is worth mentioning here that any brother of another Constitution who is elected to honorary membership should of course belong to a lodge operating under a Constitution with which the United Grand Lodge of England is in amity.

The occasions when the granting of honorary membership to a brother from another Constitution is likely to be vary rare indeed. It is however well worth mentioning here for the benefit of Brother Secretary who will undoubtedly be the person to whom the brethren will turn when and if the question arises in the lodge.

The view of Grand Lodge if your lodge operates in London or the Provincial or District office if your lodge comes under either of those authorities would be well worth taking.

Such cross-fertilisation of honorary membership is not by any means unknown and with our world appearing to shrink in size due to the speed and ease of travel, and the more frequent inter-visiting of members of foreign lodges with our own, this subject may well become more widely in vogue in the future than has been the case in the past.

Chapter 44:

The Grand Secretary's Newsletter

A relatively recent and much-needed innovation in the communication of information has been brought about by the introduction of a quarterly newsletter written by the Grand Secretary and sent to all lodge secretaries for them to distribute to their members as quickly as possible after receipt.

This newsletter is compiled immediately after each Quarterly Communication of Grand Lodge. It contains the events which formed the basis of that meeting together with such news of forthcoming appointments as are to be made by the Grand Master.

Any announcements which it is considered are required to be made to the craft in general are included within the content of this newsletter and its speedy despatch to all members of a lodge and their early reading of its contents are to be highly recommended.

Its purpose is to communicate to all members of the craft as quickly as possible such information as is considered important for them to know for the good of the craft and for their own general information of changes and appointments within the hierarchy both in Grand Lodge and within the leadership of the Provinces and Districts throughout the world.

Chapter 45:

Attendance at Grand Lodge

It is frequently the case in some lodges that junior brethren find difficulty in establishing who are and who are not members of the United Grand Lodge of England.

The answer can be given in a number of ways but perhaps it is easier to understand if it is explained that any brother who is a duly installed active Warden, any Master, any Past Master and any Past Grand Stewards who are Masters or Past Masters, are all members of Grand Lodge providing they are current fee paying members of a private lodge.

For confirmation of this statement see Rule 5 items 82 and 83 which shows the listing in order of precedence of the members of Grand Lodge.

It will be seen from reading Rule 83 that, and here we quote, 'The Master, Past Masters qualified under Rule 9 and Wardens of the Grand Stewards' Lodge and of every other private lodge', are members of Grand Lodge.

It will be noted from reading the text of Rule 5 item 83 that Past Wardens who have not progressed through the chair and thereby become duly installed Masters of their lodges are NOT members of Grand Lodge until such time as they are either appointed a Warden once more or are installed in the chair of King Solomon.

It is a feature of this ruling that there are countless numbers of brethren who hold Provincial and District rank, having served their lodges for years and been awarded such a rank, are none the less not installed masters and are therefore not members of Grand Lodge although they wear dark blue regalia.

Attendance at the Quarterly Communications of Grand Lodge is restricted to members of Grand Lodge as already outlined who are required to prove their authenticity upon entry to the meeting.

Every brother attending a meeting of Grand Lodge for the first time, possibly as a Warden will find that he is required to give his name which will be checked in the registers of Grand Lodge from the Installation return sent in by Brother Secretary and he will be required to sign a sheet of paper giving details of his name, rank and lodge name and number.

If these are found to be correct he will be given a token admitting him into Grand Lodge.

Although technically the Annual Investiture of Grand Officers each year is a meeting of Grand Lodge at which traditionally the Grand Master officiates, the admittance to this meeting is by ticket only presented by those suitably qualified.

A ballot is held for the disposal of any tickets not used by those to whom they were issued namely the brethren who are to be invested. Suitably qualified brethren who make an application for tickets generally exceed those tickets available many times over but clearly some applications are successful each year and a request for a ticket is well worth making by anyone who has a special reason for being present.

In consequence of this ever prevailing situation in which more brethren wish to attend than there is space into which to fit them the number of tickets to first time investees is restricted to three and those to brethren receiving a promotion is restricted to two.

The Grand Temple is always completely full on this most important of occasions each year, and it can be truthfully said to be an event to be remembered with great pleasure not only for those being invested but also for those witnessing the investiture.

Chapter 46:
Visiting Brethren from Overseas

Perhaps this chapter is more applicable for lodges within the London area where the majority of the visiting by brethren from overseas takes place, but there are many instances annually of brethren making visits to lodges throughout the length and breadth of England and Wales.

It is generally the case that a brother from overseas visiting this country will find himself at the enquiry counter in Freemasons' Hall in Great Queen Street where his request to visit a lodge in this country will be dealt with swiftly and courteously.

Grand Lodge is fortunate in receiving from many London lodges a permanent invitation to accept brethren from overseas at any of their meetings and the summons for such meetings are held at the enquiry desk awaiting their potential use by such a visiting brother.

A letter is normally written for the brother so visiting, introducing him to the secretary of the lodge and giving his name and as much detail as has been ascertained about the brother in question but the final proof of the authenticity of the individual is left for the lodge to undertake.

What action should the secretary take who receives such a letter of introduction signed by the Grand Secretary?

Clearly the brother has been sent by Grand Lodge and so it would appear that he has been accepted as the genuine article but after all it is your lodge that he is attempting to enter so it is your problem to ensure that he is fully qualified to do so, especially if you intend to move into degrees other than the first.

A sensible and frequently used course of action is for the Secretary to call Brother Director of Ceremonies and together with the Junior Warden they should test the visitor in all the degrees in which the lodge will be operating during the meeting.

Providing that they are satisfied with the answers they receive to the questions and tests they give him and the examination of his Grand Lodge Certificate, a check should then be made in the

Masonic Year Book to ascertain that the lodge from which he comes (providing it is of the English Constitution) is indeed a lodge meeting where he states and on the days he says.

Caution is especially necessary with brethren visiting from a country in which there is more than one Grand Lodge, but only one of which is recognised by the United Grand Lodge of England.

An obvious example is France, where the Grand Lodge of France (La Grande Loge de France) and the Grand Orient of France (Le Grand Orient de France) are both irregular and only the National Grand Lodge of France (La Grande Loge Nationale Française) is recognized.

Finally a check should be made against his signature and that shown on his Grand Lodge Certificate to see that they bear some similarity.

Do remember that signatures can and frequently do vary as the years pass and that a certificate signed twenty or thirty years ago may well bear a signature at some variance with the current signature used by the brother concerned, due often to advanced age.

If these checks prove satisfactory then the brother should be admitted unless there is a very good reason for such admission to be refused.

A final word of warning to those whose responsibility it is to test such a brother. Remember that the signs and words used in other parts of the world can vary considerably with our own and a sign or word at variance with those we use should not be considered as proof of someone masquerading as a member of the craft.

An obvious example is that the signs and words of the first and second degrees may be in the reverse order to those used in English lodges.

Further many Grand Lodges in the United States of America as well as other parts of the world owe their origins to the Grand Lodge of Scotland and as a result the signs they teach will be very different from our own.

The author remembers with some slight discomfort the severe testing he received from the Grand Master himself of the State of Maryland in 1977 when making a visit to that Grand Lodge in Baltimore.

The warmth of the reception afterwards more than made up for the testing before admission which culminated with a request for a 'dues card' a feature of American masonry which we do not copy. This is in fact a small card about the size of a credit card, often bearing the photograph of the brother concerned, with the added annotation that his dues are fully paid for the current year.

A brother from the United Grand Lodge of England intending to visit an American lodge would be well advised to carry his latest subscription receipt if only to obviate the necessity for an explanation which to the average American brother mason would sound highly unlikely if not suspicious!

Chapter 47:

Limitation on the Number of Candidates for a Ceremony

The Book of *Constitutions* Rule 168 states quite clearly that no lodge shall initiate, pass or raise more than two candidates on the same day without first obtaining a dispensation.

If in London the lodge concerned should of course apply to Grand Lodge at Freemasons' Hall in Great Queen Street. If in a Province or District directly to that masonic authority.

It is quite clear that the circumstances for granting such a dispensation would have to be of a special nature and the rule goes on to say that the special circumstances must be given.

Whilst it would be unusual if not extremely rare for a lodge to want to carry out or confer one degree on more than two candidates on the same day there is a situation where a facility can if followed allow the maximum of candidates to be put through whatever degree or degrees the Master may have decreed will be worked at a given meeting.

It is perfectly in order for a summons to read 'To Pass two of the four named candidates AB, CD, EF and GH' such wording allows for the possible absence of some of those so named but further allows the ceremony to be performed with at least two candidates participating.

This is particularly useful where a lodge has a backlog of work to transact and wishes to use the meeting available to the fullest advantage.

It is most important where this form of coverage is used in the summons, that immediately after the meeting the masonic authority to which the lodge reports is advised of what actually occurred at the meeting so that its records can be correctly notated.

Clearly lodges are autonomous in their decision processes and it is democratically correct that they should so be, thus the decision to initiate, pass or raise more than one candidate at a time is for that lodge to decide.

Candidates for any degree are possessed of specific memories of the occasions when they took their various degrees in Freemasonry and it should perhaps be borne in mind that personal ceremonies are to be welcomed and multi-candidate ceremonies should only be used when there is no other method of achieving the desires of the lodge in its membership objectives.

Chapter 48:

The Masonic Charities

There is an admirable booklet first issued by the United Grand Lodge of England in 1983. It sets out fully the details appertaining to donations, covenants, honorific offices, and the methods by which assistance may be obtained when required from each of the registered masonic charities.

Brother Secretary should, through the lodge Charity Steward, ensure that all the members of his lodge are issued with a copy of this excellent booklet particularly those members who have but recently joined the lodge through initiation or by becoming a joining member.

The modern facilities of Direct Debits, Bankers' Orders, Deposited Covenants, and Dividends and Interest on invested funds are all means by which the charities can benefit from the generosity of the membership of the craft and many of these systems will be helpful to high earning tax payers whose refunded tax will help to boost the value of each covenanted donation made over a minimum four year period.

This latest edition of the booklet is dated 1990 and a copy is now issued FREE with every copy of the Book of *Constitutions* purchased. If extra copies are required by any lodge they may be obtained from the Grand Secretary's Office free of charge.

Chapter 49:

Attendance at a Lodge by an Unattached Brother

An unattached brother is simply a member of the English craft who at the time of your contact with him is not paying a subscription to any lodge under the jurisdiction of the United Grand Lodge of England.

What then is his standing in relationship to attending a lodge either as a visitor or as a guest of a member? Rule 127 of the Book of *Constitutions* states quite clearly that such a brother must not attend any lodge more than once until he has again become a subscribing member of a lodge under the United Grand Lodge of England.

A brother who attends a lodge of which you are the secretary should append to his name in the appropriate place in which he would normally put his lodge name and number in the signature book the words 'unattached' together with the name and number of the lodge of which he was last a subscribing member.

It should be made perfectly clear that this rule does not bar a brother from attending any lodge of which he has been made an honorary member.

Brethren who have been excluded from one lodge under Rule 181 are not excluded from any other lodge of which they may be a subscribing member. Such exclusion applies only to the specific lodge so applying the rule.

Former members of the craft who have been expelled or have resigned from the craft automatically and permanently forfeit their right to attend any meeting of a lodge or lodge of instruction.

Chapter 50:

Printing and Publishing of Masonic Proceedings

The reading of Rule 177 will perhaps come as something of a surprise to the average lodge member and may well do so to Brother Secretary for the wording of this rule may appear to leave much for explanation and be far too widely drawn. It says and this quotation is taken verbatim from the Book of *Constitutions*

> "No Brother shall publish or cause to be published anything which according to the established principles of Masonry ought not to be published."

It would appear that this rule is one of those 'catch all' rules whereby virtually anything with a masonic content could be brought within it if authority so decided.

The publishing of ritual books, the printing of specialised books which give explanations of the words used in the three degrees and the Royal Arch would all appear to come within this framework and yet these books continue to be written and published without (as far as one can tell) any action on the part of Grand Lodge or Supreme Grand Chapter to stop them.

Clearly Brother Secretary may well find that he is asked by a brother just what he is and is not allowed to say especially when the subject of a centenary which is to be celebrated in a few years' time is discussed, and the lodge has delegated this enthusiastic brother to write a history of the lodge and publish it for the celebration of the special occasion.

Would you in those circumstances feel capable of answering the enquiring brother's question clearly and concisely, particularly in telling him what he can and what he cannot put in his history?

Perhaps the best way of answering this question is to suggest that the brother concerned takes the opportunity to examine a selection of similar histories which have been written over the years by other aspiring writers.

The libraries at Grand Lodge and indeed many masonic centres throughout the Constitution will have shelves of such works of effort and expertise.

Recounting a history of an individual lodge and its membership through the years together with such events as have gone to make it memorable will undoubtedly fall within the realms of what can be published.

Repeating in published form discussions and disagreements which have occurred in committees over the years together with the names of the brethren concerned may well not be allowed particularly if the brethren mentioned are still living.

In general terms, and it is important to say in the opinion of this author, anything which is to be sent for publication in a daily newspaper or periodical concerning Freemasonry should be cleared through the Grand Secretary before submission to the media outlet concerned.

Articles for masonic centre publications or inter lodge digests can with almost certainty be considered as suitable and such permission it is suggested would not be necessary. It is of course assumed that good taste and common sense would prevail in such matters.

A final word on the subject of publishing anything, always remember to ensure that your source material is checked for accuracy and if necessary omitted if you cannot be totally sure that the statement you are about to make in writing is accurate in every respect.

Chapter 51:

Replacement of a Grand Lodge Certificate

Rule 174 sub-section (f) covers a seldom-used requirement which is the sad occasion when a Grand Lodge Certificate becomes either lost or destroyed. The Grand Secretary may issue a duplicate to the brother to whom the original was issued upon payment of the fee prescribed in Rule 270.

It sometimes happens that a brother will lose his regalia case by having it stolen on public transport or indeed that he will lose it in a burglary.

Neither of these situations can be regarded as the fault of the brother concerned and the facility referred to exists to cover such situations where a brother finds himself without proof positive of his membership despite his ability to give signs and explain words.

Grand Lodge Certificates are clearly passports in many ways and the carrying of such items in regalia cases is perhaps not the wisest form of security. In general masonic visiting, such certificates are seldom asked for particularly if one is vouched for by a friend and the reader may well think it safer to keep his certificate securely locked away in his home. It may be required, however when visiting abroad.

Chapter 52:
Propositions and Notices of Motion

There occurs very frequently in lodges a situation whereby a proposition is made and duly seconded that a certain act or action be taken and for the most part such propositions are dealt with expeditiously and the matter in hand settled.

There are occasions when another brother wishes to vary, alter, change or otherwise amend the proposition already made and seconded. What course of action should now be taken to deal with the matter in hand?

The Master after ensuring that both the original proposition and its amendment have been correctly proposed and seconded should then take the amendment first and note the votes both for and against.

If the ballot for the amendment should prove to receive the majority of the votes of the members present then there would be no need to take a vote on the original proposition for it would automatically lapse, since the amendment becomes substantive.

If however the ballot were to show a minority vote for that amendment then the original proposition should be put and the decisions of both ballots should be recorded in the minutes.

Dealing now with the subject of a Notice of Motion, this is a totally different action from a normal proposition given in lodge.

Usually a Notice of Motion is given when a major change is suggested in the manner in which the lodge operates such as a move to another venue or a change in subscription rates.

The proposer requires to stand on the appropriate rising and state that he wishes to give a Notice of Motion that (and then proceed to give the detail of such notice). This does not require a seconder and there must be no discussion of the subject matter raised.

On the summons for the next meeting the full detail of the Notice of Motion given at the previous meeting must be stated starting with the words 'Pursuant to the Notice of Motion given at the meeting held on . . . Brother . . . will propose that . . .' and then the detail of that notice can be set out clearly for all to read.

By carrying out this action in such a way no member can say that something was rushed through the lodge without him having been given the occasion to say something on the matter for he will have ample time to communicate with Brother Secretary to express his views should he so desire.

Chapter 53:

Masonic Discipline

The era in which we live has brought forth the necessity for Grand Lodge to issue a small booklet on the subject of Masonic Discipline. This was first published in September 1988 with a second edition dated March 1990, and is available free from Freemasons' Hall.

This subject is mentioned here for the reason that there now falls upon the Master of a lodge (advised of course by Brother Secretary) the duty to report the details of a wide range of offences which if committed by a member of your lodge MUST be referred to higher authority. This is a mandatory instruction.

Such referrals should be made to either the Provincial or District Grand Secretary if the lodge concerned is in a Province or a District. If the lodge however is in London, or abroad and not in a District, then such reporting should be directed to the Grand Secretary at Freemasons' Hall, London.

This booklet is required reading by the secretary of every lodge under the English Constitution and from this instruction there can be no exceptions.

Offences both criminal and civil which would in former times have resulted in a brother proven guilty of such conduct removing himself from masonic sight, are today not regarded (by some members) with the degree of concern for the image and good name of the Craft which should be the constant concern of the entire membership.

Grand Lodge has produced and set out clearly for all members of the Craft to read precisely how such transgressions of the law are now dealt with by masonic authority.

There now exists a clearly laid down policy and procedure which is available to anyone both within and without the craft. It defines in precise terms those actions which will be taken upon the receipt of a report of any such offence together with such circumstances which will take their natural course thereafter.

Freemasonry has to be seen to have a procedure for dealing with those members who fail to live up to the high standards of both moral and ethical behaviour required of those who wish to become and remain members of our order.

It is the duty of every member of the craft to ensure that where any such known offence is committed and proven in court the matter is brought to the attention of the brother's lodge if he has failed to do so himself.

The Quick Reference Section

The following section has been written for easy reference to a shortened version of instructions and rules applying to the assistance most generally required by lodge secretaries.

1. THE ANNUAL RETURN TO GRAND LODGE

The purpose of this form which is sent directly to lodge secretaries is to enable an annual record to be made of the membership of the lodge, this WILL NOT include brethren who have been initiated or who have joined during the year. It is possible that this current procedure may alter in future years. The form which is sent complete with the names and totals of the membership already printed upon it also includes a stated figure of the dues outstanding for the lodge year which should be remitted to Grand Lodge.

Queries on or about this form should be directed to the Registry at the United Grand Lodge of England Great Queen Street, London WC2B 5AZ, telephone number 071-831 9811.

2. THE ANNUAL RETURN TO PROVINCIAL OR DISTRICT GRAND LODGE

The purpose of this form is to show to the Province or District a record of the membership of the lodge including its growth by virtue of Initiates and Joining members during the year, plus the reduction it may have suffered as a result of deaths, resignations or exclusions.

It also allows for the accurate calculation of the annual Provincial or District dues.

Payment of these dues becomes liable by virtue of the Provincial or District by-laws and such annual dues are fixed at the annual meeting of the Province or District.

3. BALLOTS FOR INITIATES, JOINING AND HONORARY MEMBERS

There is frequently considerable misunderstanding on the subject of taking a conjoint ballot, i.e., taking two or three ballots at the same time. The following explanation may assist those who are unsure of the correct procedure to adopt.

Grand Lodge recognise ONLY candidates, not as you might perhaps imagine candidates for Initiation, candidates for Joining and candidates for Honorary Membership. It is therefore quite in order for a ballot covering any variation of the above mentioned groupings to be carried out in one ballot.

Should there prove to be a negative vote then it is of course mandatory for individual ballots to be undertaken.

4. LODGE BY-LAWS

By-laws are of course framed upon the formation of a lodge and at its Consecration they are usually approved and a copy forwarded to the Province or District who in turn ensure that a copy is sent to Grand Lodge for its records.

It occasionally happens that a lodge wishes to alter, amend or otherwise reconstruct one or more of its by-laws.

For the unwary and perhaps inexperienced Lodge Secretary, it is always advisable to study very carefully the details given in Rule 136 before carrying out such a change.

For lodges in a Province or District, reference to the Provincial or District Grand Secretary is to be advised.

In London helpful advice is always readily available from Freemasons' Hall in Great Queen Street either by personal visit or by telephone.

Model by-laws are issued by Grand Lodge from time to time which cover everything usually required by the members and are to be recommended to any group of Brethren considering the formation of a new lodge.

The adoption of these model by-laws is strongly recommended when making major revisions to existing (and possibly outdated) by-laws.

5. CANDIDATES FROM OUTSIDE THE AREA

It is vital that Rule 158 of the Book of *Constitutions* is observed most fully when a candidate for Initiation neither lives nor works within the area in which your lodge operates.

Always ensure that you allow sufficient time for a reply to arrive to such an enquiry made under this rule.

It would be quite wrong to proceed with either reading the application form, conducting a ballot, or worse still carrying out a ceremony whilst making the assumption that in due time an acceptable reply will be received.

It will be found that a telephone call to a Provincial or District office will elucidate a helpful response to the question 'How long will an answer usually take?'

Some Provinces and Districts conduct their own enquiries by interviewing prospective candidates before replying to enquiries under Rule 158 therefore be prepared for a delay in processing any application until an affirmative reply is received.

6. CHANGING THE DAYS OF THE MEETING

The most frequent reason for wishing to change the days of a lodge meeting or meetings comes about as a result of a lodge changing its venue and finding that it has to fit in with existing vacancies.

Rule 141 is totally clear on the manner in which such a change of meeting days should be handled but if in doubt a telephone call to either Grand Lodge (if your lodge meets in London), or to the Provincial or District Grand Secretary if it meets in either of these areas will provide the necessary correct information.

Attention to Rule 141 sub section (iii) is recommended in such a circumstance together with the reminder that the by-laws of the lodge must of course be amended accordingly and approved by your reporting authority be that Grand Lodge, Provincial or District Grand Lodge.

7. CLEARANCE CERTIFICATES

This certificate is usually requested by a brother when resigning from a lodge or when he is to become a Founder or member of another Lodge. Rule 175 covers very clearly the issue of such certificates.

It is of course important that Brother Secretary communicates with Brother Treasurer before issuing such a certificate to ensure that the brother to whom it is being issued is clear of all financial liability to the lodge.

Contrary to popular belief it is not necessary for a printed form to be used, a simple statement signed by the Treasurer or Secretary is all that is required.

It is sometimes the case that a lodge to whom a former member has applied for membership makes contact and asks for a certificate of clearance for that former member, the same rules apply.

The detail contained in section (ii) of Rule 175 makes it quite clear the circumstances under which a certificate should be granted. It must not be assumed that a certificate is only issued when a brother has left the lodge having cleared his indebtedness. Should a lodge to whom he has applied for membership ask for a clearance certificate then one should be supplied stating the facts as they existed at the cessation of his membership be that good or bad.

8. COMPLETING A MEMBERSHIP APPLICATION FORM

Secretaries are well advised to consult the Book of *Constitutions* (Rule 159) when checking the correct procedure in regard to the accurate completion of this form. This is the form used when either a Candidate for Initiation, Joining or Rejoining wishes to become a member of your lodge.

In the most general of terms, provided that the candidate either lives or works within the area covered by your reporting centre you may start to process the form, so as to be able to supply the members with information about the candidate prior to the ballot at the meeting following him being proposed. The form must be read in open lodge before the ballot is taken (Rule 1645) even if it has been read on a previous occasion.

It should be remembered that to read a form and follow it with a ballot in open lodge should only be undertaken if it is certain that the person so applying for initiation will definitely be initiated within one year of the ballot proving in his favour.

To ballot for more candidates than can be initiated in a masonic season is not only wrong but it also involves much extra work for Brother Secretary to say nothing of the disappointment of the waiting candidate or candidates.

Dealing with Joining or Rejoining members is a different matter entirely and the foregoing remarks obviously do not apply.

9. DEATH OF THE MASTER

Rule 119 (a) deals very clearly with this situation.

The Senior Warden calls the meeting of the lodge but none other than a Past Master may occupy the Master's chair and conduct the ceremonies.

If the Immediate Past Master be present then it is his DUTY to officiate. Should he be unavoidably absent then the senior Past Master present should officiate.

It is important that both Grand Lodge and your own reporting base be advised immediately the death of the Master is known.

10. DISPENSATIONS

A Dispensation is a licence to depart from a rule or action and may be granted if the circumstances are provided for in the Book of *Constitutions*.

Applications should be made well in advance of the occasion for which the dispensation is required and Brother Secretary should never assume, simply because he has applied for a dispensation, that it will automatically be granted.

The reporting base for the lodge will require proof that such need exists before granting a dispensation to vary a fixed rule or By-law.

Always ensure that the fullest details are given when applying for a dispensation and remember that a fee is frequently charged for this service.

A Dispensation must be read in open lodge prior to the reading of the Minutes, not before the lodge is opened, and the fact must be entered in the Minutes.

11.   EXCLUSION FROM THE LODGE

A brother may be excluded for a number of reasons as examination of Rule 181 will show.

It is quite permissible for a lodge under its by-laws to enact that a period of less than the two years in Rule 148 will provide grounds for exclusion.

There are several other reasons why a brother can be excluded from membership of a lodge and it is advisable to study Rules 127, 150, 163, 180, 181, 182 and 183.

It is not necessary to learn these by heart, simply to know where to look if the occasion should arise.

Whilst dealing with the subject of removing a brother's right to membership of a lodge it should perhaps be mentioned here that only Grand Lodge possesses the right to expel a brother (Rule 4).

12.   HONORARY MEMBERS

Rule 167 of the Book of *Constitutions* adequately covers this subject but lodge secretaries are recommended to speak in confidence to brethren who are being proposed for this honour.

Although in many cases it quite rightly recognises years of service to the lodge suggesting the honour, it does at the same time bring into being certain other factors which are not always appreciated by the intended recipient of such an honour.

Membership of only one lodge (often the lodge suggesting honorary membership) means that upon being elected to such honorary membership the brother concerned automatically ceases to pay an annual fee to Grand Lodge by virtue of his no longer paying lodge dues, a proportion of which goes to Grand Lodge on his behalf.

He thereby becomes unattached and is therefore only able to visit any other lodge in the English Constitution once (except other lodges of which he may be an honorary member).

This does of course not apply to brethren who are members of more than one lodge.

The election to honorary membership of a brother relieves the lodge so electing him of the ongoing responsibility to pay an annual fee to Grand Lodge or to the Province or District in which the lodge meets, on behalf of that brother.

This however is not true of the year in which he is elected or any part of it when the annual fees must be paid in full.

Honorary membership is not an honour to be awarded lightly or without much thought and discussion and it must be seen to have been earned in every sense of the word and not simply be a means of relieving an elderly brother of paying a subscription to his lodge.

13.   INSTALLATION RETURN TO GRAND LODGE

The purpose of this form is two-fold, firstly it advises the United Grand Lodge of England of the names of the Master and Wardens installed in office for the ensuing year, and secondly it advises the names of the Past Masters both of and in the lodge who are current in membership and thereby entitled to attend the Quarterly Communications of Grand Lodge.

It is vitally important that this form is signed by the newly Installed Master on the night of his Installation and returned to the Grand Secretary as quickly as possible after the day of the Installation meeting. Failure to do so could well mean that anyone named on that form presenting themselves at the porch of Grand Lodge could be refused admission.

14.   LONDON — PROVINCIAL — DISTRICT GRAND RANK

Appointment to Senior London Grand Rank and London Grand Rank is given at the discretion of the Grand Master and his decision may not be questioned.

Provincial or District Grand Rank is given at the hand of the Provincial or District Grand Master whose decision also may not be questioned.

In London recommendation forms are sent on a regular basis which allow the Past Masters of the lodge to recommend a suitably qualified and worthy brother for the honour of London Grand Rank.

Recommendations for promotion to Senior London Grand Rank may be submitted to the Grand Secretary by lodges having a suitable and worthy candidate.

Such applications should give the fullest details of the brother so recommended and his particular attributes which justify such an application.

It should be remembered that a Past Master should not be recommended for London Grand Rank until a full five years have passed after his Mastership is concluded (i.e. he has left the chair).

Likewise a recommendation for Senior London Grand Rank on behalf of a brother holding London Grand Rank will equally not be considered until a period of five years has passed after his having been granted his original rank.

Each Province and District operates its own system in regard to the awarding of such local rank and it would be invidious to attempt an explanation of the various systems in use.

In general those brethren appointed to Active or Past Provincial Rank are selected by the Province or District after a given period following mastership of their lodge. This can vary from five to ten years depending upon the size of the Province or District.

Promotions within Provinces and Districts are given once again usually after a pre-determined period has passed.

Brother Secretary has a duty to bring to the attention of either the Grand Secretary or the Provincial or District Grand Secretary the details of any brother whom he considers has been either unfairly treated or has been passed over for no apparent reason. A response will always be forthcoming and this should be retained for future reference as if it achieves nothing else it does show that you had the constant care and fair treatment of all your brethren very much in mind throughout your period as secretary of the lodge.

15. MINUTES OF A LODGE MEETING

Although to the experienced lodge secretary the requirement to take Minutes at a lodge meeting appears obvious he may not be aware that this is a mandatory requirement of Rule 144 of the Book of *Constitutions* which specifies the items that must be included.

Fortunately the rule does not specify the format to which such minutes should conform. Brother Secretary therefore has a certain licence to use his initiative in the compilation and recording of the events of the meeting.

A final word on this subject. Minutes should record appointments made, elections decided, propositions put, decisions arrived at and actions taken. Be long and specific enough to give an accurate word picture of the meeting, and yet not so long as to be boring to the listener be he member or visitor.

16. MOVING TO ANOTHER VENUE

The likelihood of this occurring to the majority of lodges is slight and precisely because of this fact it sometimes becomes a minefield for the unwary.

Rule 141 is quite explicit and the inexperienced secretary in particular is recommended most highly to study it before embarking upon any action. If he is in any doubt he should contact Grand Lodge if in London or his Provincial or District Grand Secretary if that applies.

The timing of such Notices of Motion and their subsequent necessary voting implications should always be borne in mind.

Finally remember that a change of venue will ALWAYS require a change in the by-laws of the lodge.

17. NON-PAYMENT OF SUBSCRIPTIONS

It is incumbent upon the Lodge Secretary to notify both Grand Lodge and Provincial or District Grand Lodge of the name and period of indebtedness of a brother who fails to pay his subscription for a period of two years. His membership ceases automatically (Rule 148, Book of *Constitutions*).

It is a requirement of this rule that the fact be announced at the next regular meeting of the lodge and recorded in the minutes.

The name of the former member who subsequently pays all his indebtedness to the lodge and once again resumes membership by rejoining should be communicated to Grand Lodge and Provincial or District Grand Lodge in order that the fact be recorded accurately in their files.

18. PASSING AND RAISING CANDIDATES FROM ANOTHER LODGE

It is perfectly permissible for lodges to Pass and Raise candidates from other lodges providing that due observance has been paid to Rule 173 (a).

Such ceremonies as are conducted under this rule must be notified to Grand Lodge and Provincial or District Grand Lodge as well as the lodge in which the brother concerned was initiated.

19. INTERVAL BETWEEN DEGREES

As will quickly be seen from reading Rule 172 the period of time between the conferring of the degrees must be four weeks.

Where a lodge experiences a backlog of degrees to perform it is perfectly possible for another lodge to be asked to carry out a degree of Passing or Raising providing the requirements of Rule 173 have been met.

It should be mentioned here that a dispensation can be obtained to vary Rule 172 in circumstances of necessity.

20. PERIOD BETWEEN PROPOSAL AND BALLOTING

The membership application form containing the details of the prospective member for initiation or joining must be deposited with the secretary of the lodge prior to the regular meeting at which the member is to be proposed (Rule 159 refers).

A lodge may specify in its by-laws that an application shall be deposited with the Secretary for a reasonable number of days before such meeting (see Rule 164 (c)).

Once a candidate for Initiation, Joining or Rejoining has been proposed and seconded in lodge, it is mandatory that the ballot for that candidate or candidates be taken at the next regular meeting of the lodge, that the details are entered on the summons for that meeting and that application be read in lodge prior to the ballot (see Rules 159 and 164).

If a candidate is not initiated within one year after his election, such election becomes void and the whole procedure must be re-enacted if it is still desired to proceed with the application.

21. POSTPONEMENT OF AN INSTALLATION
MEETING

Rule 108 (a) deals with this situation in a clear and precise manner and Brother Secretary is recommended to study this rule carefully.

Remember that the Master of a lodge remains in office until such time as he is replaced by the installation of a new Master.

It is important that the details of a postponement of an installation meeting are communicated to your reporting base be that Grand Lodge or Provincial or District Grand Lodge.

It should be remembered that there is another factor which must be dealt with if the lodge be in a Province or a District where it is a regular feature of installation meetings for a representative to attend on behalf of the Provincial or District Grand Master.

Clearly it is vital that this dignitary is advised as quickly as possible of the circumstances prevailing and he can then make a decision regarding his own attendance.

22. PRESENTATION OF A GRAND LODGE CERTIFICATE

As will be appreciated by the reading of Rule 174 (d) a brother's Grand Lodge Certificate should be presented to him in open lodge and the fact entered in the minutes.

Where it is not possible for any reason for this to be done, the Certificate should be sent to him by registered post and the secretary should report this fact at the next regular lodge meeting so that it can be duly recorded in the minutes.

It is quite wrong for the secretary to retain the Certificate of a newly raised brother in the hope that he may attend some future meeting of the lodge and that the certificate can be presented on that occasion.

He is ENTITLED to receive this certificate as proof of his having taken the three degrees in Craft masonry and it should not be withheld from him for any reason whatsoever.

A Grand Lodge Certificate MUST be signed in the margin provided by the brother to whom it is issued immediately after its presentation in Lodge. Where a Certificate is sent by post the brother to whom it is directed should be instructed to sign it immediately upon receipt.

23. REGISTER OF MEMBERS

Rule 146 (ii) requires every lodge to keep a register of all its members both Present and Past together with dates of Initiation, Passing and Raising, or Joining or Rejoining as the case may be together with their ages, addresses, titles, professions or occupations, and the dates and reasons for their ceasing to be members.

In addition to the foregoing Brother Secretary will find it of considerable use also to have a record of the offices held by each member in the lodge and the year that such office was held.

24. REQUESTING A GRAND LODGE CERTIFICATE

When a candidate has been Initiated and the application form has been sent to Grand Lodge complete with the appropriate registration fee, the only subsequent action to be taken by the lodge secretary is for the completion of the form setting out details of the dates the said brother was passed and raised.

The timing of the production and receipt by the secretary of a Grand Lodge Certificate varies according to the time of year but a period of four weeks is not unusual.

If the Certificate is required for presentation at a special meeting a letter accompanying the request setting out that date will undoubtedly receive the co-operatio
n required.

25.   SUSPENSION OR RESIGNATION FROM A LODGE

Secretaries are thoroughly recommended to study most carefully the details contained in Rules 179 and 183 of the Book of *Constitutions*, for the miscellany of ways in which this particular action can be dealt with are a masonic minefield for the unwary.

It is important that Brother Secretary makes a note of the date on which he received either orally or in writing a resignation from a brother for this may well have an important bearing on subsequent actions.

26.   RESPONSIBILITY FOR THE FEES FOR INITIATION OR JOINING

The attention of ALL proposers and seconders should be directed towards the provisions of Rule 171 which quite clearly states that any member who proposes or seconds a candidate for Initiation or Joining shall be responsible to the lodge for all fees payable under its by-laws in respect of such candidate.

This does not necessarily mean that they have to pay such fees themselves, simply that they are responsible for seeing that such fees are paid.

27.   RESPONSIBILITY FOR THE LODGE OF INSTRUCTION

It is frequently not appreciated that a lodge of instruction operates under the sanction of the lodge itself and that responsibility for the lodge of instruction and its correct behaviour rests with the lodge members.

It is occasionally the case that a lodge of instruction behaves as though it has the power to make changes to its constitution and format, such however is not the case and reference to Rules 132, 133, 134 and 135 will clearly indicate the true facts applying to every lodge of instruction and its responsibilities.

Any change of venue MUST be approved at a regular lodge meeting after due notification on the summons.

ALL meeting places for lodges of instruction have to be approved, be they in London, the Provinces or Districts and none may be used until sanction has been received approving their suitability.

28.   VACANCY OF A LODGE OFFICER

A frequently-held belief, albeit quite a wrong one, is that if an officer of the lodge should die or become unable to execute his office for the remainder of the year then that office cannot be filled until the next Installation meeting.

This is quite wrong as reference to Rule 121 will quickly show.

The foregoing information does NOT apply to the Master of the lodge.